P9-DDW-228

"As a pastor, I think regularly about what [...] have after I am with the Lord and occupied with other things. [...] generational transition in church leadership are among the greatest a church will ever face. With that in mind, I welcome Thabiti Anyabwile's fine contribution to this necessary discussion. *Finding Faithful Elders and Deacons* promises to be a great help indeed."

Douglas Wilson, Fellow of Philosophy and Classic Languages,
New St. Andrews College; Pastor, Christ Church, Moscow, Idaho

"Choosing men who will lead your church is serious work. I commend this valuable resource to you from my friend and partner in the gospel Thabiti Anyabwile. It is both thoughtful and practical. His insights in this book will help you recruit, enlist, and reproduce faithful leaders in your church."

James MacDonald, Senior Pastor, Harvest Bible Chapel,
Rolling Meadows, Illinois

"Out of an obvious love for the local church, Pastor Thabiti takes biblical leadership very seriously. He takes it so seriously that he has written a book designed to be both biblical and accessible to the people of the church—clearly explaining the Bible's teaching on the qualifications for leadership and so much more. After a careful exposition of every leadership qualification, he includes a list of helpful questions for the aspiring leader to ask himself and for those who will be interviewing such aspiring leaders. Thank you, Thabiti, for helping me to reflect more deeply on my calling as an elder and in my effort to raise up God-glorifying and people-loving leaders in Christ's church for the next generation!"

Tom Steller, Pastor for Leadership Development,
Bethlehem Baptist Church, Minneapolis, Minnesota;
Dean, Bethlehem College and Seminary

"How do we identify, pick, and train the leaders we so desperately need? Pastor Thabiti has written a practical and theologically faithful book that addresses this critical issue, leaving no stone unturned. It is the kind of book you will want to keep on hand and refer to as you consider potential deacons and elders for the ministry. The book is down to earth, relevant, and thought provoking."

Dave Kraft, Pastor, Mars Hill Church, Orange County;
author, *Leaders Who Last*

"Thabiti Anyabwile's book is a great reminder of the basics that can easily be forgotten in the race for ecclesiastical progress—namely, that we need faithful elders and deacons. Although this book is meant to help those looking for church officers know what to look for, I found the questions to be a good tonic to my soul and a mirror exposing the areas in which I need to shape up as a church pastor."

Conrad Mbewe, Pastor, Kabwata Baptist Church, Lusaka, Zambia;
author, *Foundations for the Flock*

"This is a great book. On the surface, it's an extended meditation on the biblical qualities of elders and deacons that causes you to think carefully about what God intends for his leaders. What should churches look for? Are you that kind of person? But underneath, it's a radical reorientation of what leadership in the church is. Church leadership does not depend on academic or professional success but on godliness. This book will help change the way church members and leaders think of leadership, what they value, and what they cultivate. Leaders and members both will benefit."

Jonathan Leeman, Editorial Director, 9Marks;
author, *The Church and the Surprising Offense of God's Love* and
Reverberation

"*Finding Faithful Elders and Deacons* offers the sort of meditations from the Pastoral Epistles that would-be elders and deacons-in-training need. Yet, pastors and laymen alike will find these chapters to be insightful and poignant, for they are faithful to Scripture, culturally contextualized, and able to be implemented instantly. There are thousands of well-meaning churches peddling along with mediocre religious practice that could be transformed into vibrant, Christ-pleasing, soul-winning, community-transforming churches if the officers of their congregations would humbly embrace the simple exhortations of this gracious work."

Eric C. Redmond, Senior Pastor, Reformation Alive Baptist Church,
Temple Hills, Maryland

"As a member of a pastoral team that is always at some point in the process of identifying, developing, and affirming elders and deacons, I welcome this helpful book by Thabiti Anyabwile. Right from the start, with the simple clarity and conviction of its opening sentences, this book is marked by sound biblical teaching. The consistent transition into the practical counsel at the end of each chapter, however, is where this book really proves its worth. *Finding Faithful Elders and Deacons* will be a most useful primer for all those who are committed to doing church leadership by the Bible."

Mike Bullmore, Senior Pastor, Crossway Community Church,
Bristol, Wisconsin

FINDING FAITHFUL ELDERS AND DEACONS

OTHER CROSSWAY BOOKS in the IX Marks Series:

Church Planting Is for Wimps: How God Uses Messed-up People to Plant Ordinary Churches That Do Extraordinary Things, Mike McKinley (2010)

What Does God Want of Us Anyway?: A Quick Overview of the Whole Bible, Mark Dever (2010)

What Is the Gospel?, Greg Gilbert (2010)

It Is Well: Expositions on Substitutionary Atonement, Mark Dever and Michael Lawrence

Biblical Theology in the Life of the Church: A Guide for Ministry, Michael Lawrence (2010)

The Church and the Surprising Offense of God's Love, Jonathan Leeman (2010)

What Is a Healthy Church Member?, Thabiti Anyabwile (2008)

What Is a Healthy Church?, Mark Dever (2007)

The Gospel and Personal Evangelism, Mark Dever (2007)

FINDING FAITHFUL ELDERS AND DEACONS

✛

THABITI M. ANYABWILE

:: CROSSWAY

WHEATON, ILLINOIS

Library of Congress Cataloging-in-Publication Data
Anyabwile, Thabiti M., 1970–
Finding faithful elders and deacons / Thabiti Anyabwile.
    p. cm.
    Includes index.
    ISBN 978-1-4335-2992-4 (tp)
    1. Elders (Church officers)—Baptists. 2. Deacons—Baptists.
I. Title.
BX6345.A59   2012
253—dc23   2011037801

In memory of Philip Pedley,
faithful elder and servant,
who honored Jesus

CONTENTS

Introduction   11

How to Use This Book   15

PART ONE

FINDING TABLE SERVANTS

1   Choosing Your Waiter: An Introduction to Deacons   19

2   Full of the Spirit and Wisdom   23

3   Sincere   27

4   Sober and Content   31

5   Keeps Hold of the Faith   35

6   Tried and True   41

PART TWO

FINDING RELIABLE ELDERS

7   Sheep and Shepherds: An Introduction to Elders   47

8   Desires a Noble Task   51

9   Above Reproach   57

10   A One-Woman Man   61

11   Sober-Minded, Self-Controlled, Respectable   67

12   Hospitable   71

13   Able to Teach   77

14   Sober, Gentle, Peacemaking   83

15   Not a Lover of Money   87

16   Leader at Home   95

17   Mature and Humble   99

18   Respected by Outsiders   105

PART THREE

WHAT GOOD PASTORS DO

19	Elders Refute Error	111
20	Elders Avoid Myths and Train for Godliness	117
21	Elders Hope in God	123
22	Elders Command	127
23	Elders Let No One Despise Their Youth	131
24	Elders Set an Example	135
25	Elders Teach	141
26	Elders Grow	145
27	Elders Watch Their Life	151
28	Elders Watch Their Doctrine	155
Afterword		161
Appendix: Sample Elder Ordination Vows		163
Notes		165
General Index		167
Scripture Index		171

INTRODUCTION

And what you have heard from me in the presence of many witnesses entrust to faithful men who will be able to teach others also.

2 TIMOTHY 2:2

A church without godly leaders is an endangered church. And a church that does not train leaders is an unfaithful church. God gives leaders to his churches for the maturity, unity, and soundness of each local congregation. Without godly, faithful, replicating leadership, churches suffer deeply.

The apostle Paul knew how important such leadership is. In 2 Timothy, the apostle writes his "child" in the faith, Timothy, with several final instructions and exhortations, including the exhortation to find good leaders. Timothy grew up under the spiritual instruction of his grandmother Lois and mother Eunice (2 Tim. 2:2, 5). He traveled, served, and learned alongside Paul. And now the apostle, near the end of his life, instructing in the "shadow of the scaffold,"[1] writes with deep tenderness in almost every verse. Amidst the many jewels in this letter, one of them is Paul's charge to find and entrust "faithful men."

The apostle's teaching must live on, passed from faithful hand to faithful hand. That means that the pastor must be able to spot faithful men and train them. If a man is not given to discipling others, it's unlikely that he is called to the pastoral office.

I am the product of men who found me, probed my reliability, and entrusted me with gospel treasure. I think of Peter Rochelle. He selflessly granted me the opportunity to labor alongside him in

11

planting a church. He first encouraged me to preach and teach, and his model of exposition has influenced me ever since.

Then there was Mark Dever, an unusually gifted discipler of men and teacher of God's Word. I cannot forget his eager generosity towards me. It began on the day of my membership interview at Capitol Hill Baptist Church. He asked what I wanted to do with my life over the long term. A little intimidated, I answered, "I would love it if the Lord allowed me to pastor full-time."

"Really?" Mark replied, eyebrow curiously raised, head slightly tilted. Then he turned to my wife and asked, "Can he teach?"

Oh no, I thought. *I did not see that coming. What would she say?* To my relief, "Oh, yes," came the quick and confident reply. Mark turned to me and said, "You should call the church office and get on my calendar for regular lunches together. Let's meet up and discuss good Christian books. You should consider my life open to you."

I have never forgotten those words. My five years at Capitol Hill Baptist Church were marked by Mark, Michael Lawrence, Matt Schmucker, and too many men to number—not to mention the church family as a whole—pouring themselves into me, entrusting me with the things they had heard, read, seen, and learned concerning the Lord, the gospel, and his bride.

WHAT DO MULTI-LEVEL MARKETERS HAVE THAT CHRISTIAN CHURCHES DO NOT?

For a number of years, every time I visited a bookstore I seemed to be approached by someone who asked me if I was interested in "earning an extra $500 to $1,000 per month working from home only ten hours per week." It was like I had a big sticker on my forehead reading "sucker for multi-level marketing." They wanted me to become a part of their "down line"—to join their league of unsuspecting, gullible, get-rich-quick marketers. They were multiplying themselves in the most zealous way possible.

What do multi-level marketers possess that Christian pastors do not?

If direct sale and multi-level marketing businesses are constantly on the lookout for prospective representatives, certainly ambassadors for Christ should be. We've been entrusted with the ministry of reconciliation. Having come into possession of Christ himself, it's our business and pleasure to cultivate other stewards of God's good news, stewards who will in turn find others to keep and teach the gospel.

But *saying* that a pastor must find and train others is the easy part. Practically, what does this look like? How is it done?

In the chapters that follow, I want to invite pastors and elders to a conversation about finding and training faithful men for the task of leadership in the church. I am no expert. I haven't been at this long, and I'm sure there are tons of men who do it better. You won't find here a ten-step process for turning spiritual duds into elder studs. You won't find a surefire formula for making any and every person a stellar leader.

Instead, what follows are brief meditations on Paul's instructions to Timothy in 1 Timothy 3 and 4. With 1 Timothy 3, we examine the biblical qualifications for elders and deacons and ask, what kind of character must these men possess, and how can we spot it? With 1 Timothy 4, we consider Paul's charge to Timothy as a model for faithful pastoral ministry. With God's blessing, as we walk slowly through 1 Timothy 3 and 4, we will think about what qualities to search for and what duties need to be fulfilled in Christian leadership.

Much more could be said on this very important topic. Many excellent book-length resources are available to the interested reader.[2] I hope this little volume complements these other resources by helping the already-stretched pastor who wants to cultivate other leaders but needs a conversation partner to stir up some questions and ideas.

HOW TO USE THIS BOOK

HOW CAN YOU USE THIS BOOK?

First, use this book prayerfully. Pray for pastors and elders as they shepherd and serve the sheep. Pray for more men to be raised up in the congregation for this important work. Pray that the Lord would pour out his grace on those serving in these tasks. Pray that the members of the church would show genuine appreciation, love, and care for their shepherds. Pray that all the men in the church would grow in the qualities that elders should possess. Pray that men would have a godly desire to give their lives in serving the body of Christ as servant-leaders.

Second, use this book practically. The book does not delve into a lot of detailed argumentation, hoping instead to make application easily and quickly. I want the book to help in actually *doing* something—identifying and training elders—not just considering something. Put the suggestions into practice, and improve them with the experience and wisdom that come from your particular church setting and other faithful leaders.

Finally, use the book pedagogically. That is, use it to teach and instruct. Perhaps a church needs to select its first elders after a period of planning and study. Pastors may wish to use these brief chapters to "flesh out" for the average church member which qualities the congregation as a whole needs to be looking and praying for in their prospective elders. Examination and pastoral search committees may find similar help.

HOW NOT TO USE THIS BOOK

This book is not a sourcebook for leading witch hunts and rebellions against leaders. Shepherds are not perfect men. Though God sets the bar for pastoral ministry necessarily high, he uses the poles of grace to support that bar.

Users should keep the Lord's grace in mind as they read, lest an overly critical, gospel-forgetting, judgmental attitude develop. Few things are as harmful as the Lord's people becoming censorious toward the Lord's under-shepherds. In fact, the Bible itself tells us that rebellion against our spiritual leaders is of no advantage to us (Heb. 13:17). I very much hope this series of brief meditations would be an advantage for both pastors and people.

May the Lord be pleased to use this volume to help us recognize the gifts he has already given to his body for our growth in Christ (Eph. 4:11–16).

Thabiti M. Anyabwile
Grand Cayman, Cayman Islands
October 12, 2010

PART ONE

FINDING TABLE SERVANTS

1

CHOOSING YOUR WAITER: AN INTRODUCTION TO DEACONS

✠

I frequent restaurants fairly often. It's where a good deal of one-on-one discipleship happens. I meet with men from the church to discuss the Scripture, our lives, and good Christian books. Aside from the joy of sharing a meal together, having a good waiter helps make these visits fruitful. When waiters enjoy their task as table servers, when they are eager to serve, when they are available but not intrusive, then the experience is quite enjoyable.

The downside, of course, is that restaurant patrons generally don't get to choose their waiters. We arrive, are seated by a host or hostess, and then wait for whichever waiter has been assigned to our zone. We may find ourselves served by a wonderful waiter. But we may not. The server may not know the menu very well, could be experiencing a bad day, might have poor skills, or may be arriving from another table where he or she was treated badly. In secular speak, getting a good waiter is "the luck of the draw."

You might not have realized it, but there is at least one aspect of life in the local church that is like eating a meal in a restaurant. The local church, too, has table servers. We call them "deacons." The joy, peace, unity, and fruitfulness of the local church depends in part on having a cadre of faithful table servants who are present when needed, eager to serve without being intrusive.

The next several chapters focus on finding deacons in the local church—faithful table servers who give themselves to caring for the needs of the body. In the last decade or two, more and more churches have adopted the biblical model of eldership, which means the deacon role has either been redefined or neglected. But deacons are an indispensable part of serving the body of Christ and of multiplying the church's ministry.

We see this quite clearly in Acts 6, where the apostles charge the church in Jerusalem to find several men full of the Spirit and wisdom. The word *deacons* is not used in this passage, but the passage seems to point in this direction.

The opportunity: Acts 6:1 points out that "the disciples were increasing in number." It was a time of spiritual prosperity in the conversion of souls and enrollment in the school of Christ. The Word of God was advanced and produced much fruit.

The threat: Inside the church, however, the Greek or Greek-speaking Jews lodged a complaint against the Hebraic or Hebrew-speaking Jews. The former group didn't believe food was distributed equally among their widows. Nor did this unequal distribution appear to randomly occur. It looked as if the widows were being treated differently because they were either Greeks or Hebrews. It seemed that cultural or ethnic prejudice was threatening the unity of the church and the physical well-being of some members.

The solution: so the apostles did two things. First, they determined to prioritize their own ministry of the Word and prayer, over caring for physical needs. Second, they instructed the church to choose seven men to "serve tables"—to deacon (v. 2). In doing so, the apostles made provision for both the ministry of the Word and the ministry of the widows.

To modern sensibilities, "serving tables" sometimes connotes a low-level, demeaning position. A person waits tables when he or she is working through college, or passing time until a career takes off. People regard it as a necessary sacrifice to make ends meet.

But how different it is in the Lord's church! The apostles under the inspiration of God's Spirit appear to have created an entirely new office in the church for the specific purpose of serving tables. And the loftiness of the office is seen in (a) the character of the individuals required to fill it ("full of the Spirit and of wisdom" v. 3), (b) the fact that it facilitates the ministry of Word and prayer, and (c) the unifying and strengthening effect it has on the whole church. The deaconate is important!

Are there widows in our churches who are not well cared for? Perhaps we need to consider our work with deacons. Are there inequities in the distribution of benevolence resources in the church? Sounds like a job for deacons.

Are there cultural tensions and threats to unity in the church? Do we wish to see a more diverse church integrated in Christian life? The position of deacon was established to promote harmony across cultural and language lines.

Is the church threatened by a possible split? Deacons were the early church's "shock absorbers."[3] They absorbed complaints and concerns, resolved them in godliness, and so preserved the unity and witness of the saints.

When Stephen, Philip, Prochorus, Nicanor, Timon, Parmenas, and Nicolaus were commissioned for the deaconate, "the word of God spread" and "the number of disciples in Jerusalem increased rapidly, and a large number of priests became obedient to the faith" (Acts 6:7 NIV). Who among us would not like to see the Word spread, the number of disciples rapidly increase, and *large numbers* of people become obedient to the faith? An effective deacon ministry facilitated this in the early church since it freed the deacons of the Word—the apostles—to do their work. With this hope in mind, I pray the Lord would guide us in our consideration of deacons and how to find them.

2

FULL OF THE SPIRIT AND WISDOM

Therefore, brothers, pick out from among you seven men of good repute, full of the Spirit and of wisdom, whom we will appoint to this duty.

ACTS 6:3

⊕

Because God is gracious and kind, he has allowed me to serve in pastoral ministry as an elder and senior pastor for several years now. The longer the Lord allows me to serve in pastoral ministry, the deeper he impresses upon me the importance of praying for faithful men to serve as deacons in the church.

At a recent members' meeting, the congregation celebrated the ministry of a brother ending his term as our deacon of personnel. At the time, our deacon headed the country's largest telecom corporation. He was a very busy man. Yet person after person remembered him for his humility, spiritual focus, eagerness to serve, and wisdom.

The congregation's thanksgiving reminded me of the Spirit-given wisdom and insight of the apostles in Acts 6. The apostles instructed the young and rapidly growing church in Jerusalem to "pick out from among you seven men of good repute, full of the Spirit and of wisdom" (v. 3). Our deacon of personnel certainly met those qualifications, and all churches need such men.

When looking for deacons, churches must look for men full of the Spirit. The office is a spiritual office. Its discharge is a spiritual work, even if your church organizes deacons around specific practical tasks. The church and the gospel receive no advantage from our appointing those who are not full of the Spirit. Deacons are to be men known to be full of the Spirit and wisdom.

QUESTIONS AND OBSERVATIONS

1) Does the prospective deacon have a reputation for being filled with the Spirit and wisdom?

The apostles recommended men who were *known* for these characteristics. They did not recommend taking chances on people of unproven character. Deacons must be people who are controlled by God's Spirit rather than their own flesh or sinful nature. Moreover, the office requires people who live in the fear of the Lord, which is the beginning of wisdom (Prov. 1:7). Deacons should be people who know how to live by God's precepts, and apply them to life's situations. That is the essence of wisdom. So ask, does the prospective deacon have the reputation of keeping in step with God's Spirit and living wisely before the Lord?

2) Does the person put the ministry of the Word and prayer above the practical needs of the church?

The primary purpose for which the apostles appointed deacons was to make sure the ministry of the Word was not neglected. Therefore, you want to make sure that the potential deacon understands his role as an opportunity to free up the ministry of the Word and prayer, not to compete with it. Does he recognize the facilitating aspect of his role, or is he an advocate for more attention to this or that practical need? Martyn Lloyd-Jones, commenting on Acts 6:3, noted three ways in which the deacon must recognize the priority of spiritual matters and the ministry of the Word:

> It is wrong to put "serving tables" before the preaching of the Word of God because it is always wrong to put man before God. That, in a nutshell, is the real trouble with the world. Man is at the center; man is everything. . . .

24

So it is wrong to put man before God, and, second, in exactly the same way, it is wrong to put the body before the soul. In other words, we are not only wrong about God, we are wrong about man. What is man? According to the modern theory, man is only body, and so you must attend to everything to do with the body; give it plenty of food, plenty of drink, clothing, shelter, medical care, plenty of sex. Oh, the tragedy that humanity should think it is complimenting itself and exalting itself by turning its back upon God to concentrate on physical needs. And this is what this Word of God encounters, what it denounces. . . .

Finally, is it not the height of folly and indeed the greatest tragedy to put time before eternity? The feeding of the body only belongs to time. A day is coming in the life of all of us when we will not be interested in food, and when food will not be able to help us at all; we will be beyond that.[4]

A solid deacon prioritizes God over man, the soul over the body, and eternity over time even while he attends to the important practical and bodily needs of people.

3) Is he a servant?

Though our culture thinks of table service as demeaning and lowly, we Christians should not miss the fact that such lowliness and willingness to serve reflects Christ's life and humility. He came to serve, not to be served, and to give his life as a ransom (Mark 10:45). He made himself of no reputation, humbled himself, and took on the form of a bondservant (Phil. 2:3–8). Does the potential deacon see service as a necessary part of following Christ? Is he happy to accept menial tasks and duties that lack glamor? Or, does he want applause and recognition and attention for "his" ministries?

4) Does he evidence the fruit of the Spirit (Gal. 5:22–23)?

You want to ask whether the virtues of love, joy, peace, patience, kindness, goodness, faithfulness, gentleness, and self-control are evident in how someone serves and in his general conduct. Deacons attend to any number of thorny frustrations and problems in the local church. So, they need to be people full of grace, able to address issues with the Spirit's power and qualities. They should be able to "keep in step with the Spirit" and "not become conceited, provoking and envying" others (Gal. 5:25–26 NIV). Potential deacons should not stir up strife but settle it. So ask, is the person a talebearer or is he able to keep appropriate confidences? Does he know how to end murmuring and complaining? Do others feel genuinely loved and gently treated when interacting with him?

5) Does he demonstrate Spirit-inspired wisdom?
Not only must a deacon resolve problems, but he also must be able to anticipate problems so that the unavoidable bumps along the way do not completely derail the church in its mission. To do this well, a person needs wisdom. Is the potential deacon known for his discernment, insight, and sound judgment when interacting with people? Is he known for wisdom when addressing problems? Is he slow to speak, quick to listen, and slow to become angry (James 1:19–20)? Does he consider the ideas of others, or is he committed to his own thoughts more than others' (Phil. 2:3)? Does he show wisdom in not only arriving at decisions but also in implementing and helping others to understand the decision?

CONCLUSION
One cannot overestimate the importance of Spirit-filled persons serving in the office of deacon. If the apostles themselves—men with unique calling and gifts—saw the crucial importance of having Spirit-filled Christians serve in this way, how much more do we need such partners in the gospel? Learning to identify and pray for such people strengthens our local congregations.

3

SINCERE

Deacons likewise must be dignified, not double-tongued, not addicted to much wine, not greedy for dishonest gain.

1 TIMOTHY 3:8

⊕

Having narrowly escaped Vanity Fair, John Bunyan's hero, Christian, in *Pilgrim's Progress* falls into the company of a certain Mr. By-ends from the town of Fairspeech. Christian questions By-ends about the town and By-ends assures Christian that Fairspeech includes wealthy and noble people. He mentions a list of his relatives residing in Fairspeech:

> Almost the whole town. In particular, My Lord Turn-about, my Lord Timeserver, my Lord Fairspeech, from whose ancestors that town first took its name; also Mr. Smoothman, Mr. Facing-both-ways and Mr. Anything. And the parson of our parish, Mr. Two-tongues, was my mother's own brother by her father's side. And, to tell you the truth, I have become a gentleman of good quality, yet my great-grandfather was only a waterman, looking one way and rowing another. And I got most of my estate by the same occupation.[5]

The gentry of Bunyan's fictional Fairspeech all suffer from the plague of insincere speech.

DEACONS AND SINCERITY

How would you like to live in a town with a parson deservedly known as "Mr. Two-tongues"? However well respected such persons may be among people sharing in their habit of flattery and half-truths, Bunyan's Mr. Two-tongues would never be a suitable candidate for the office of deacon.

Why?

Not only should deacons be men full of the Holy Spirit, but it follows that they should also be "dignified" or "sincere" (NIV). Deacons must not be "double-tongued" or "two-faced" or "indulging in double talk." They must mean what they say and say what they mean. They must avoid the sin of flattery and speak the truth in love.

People may be double-tongued in two ways. They may say one thing to one person and another thing to someone else. Or, they may *say* one thing but *do* another. In either case, forked tongues make such people unreliable and unqualified for serving as deacons. A deacon's "yes" must be yes, and his "no" no (2 Cor. 1:17–18).

Sincerity reflects the character of Christ. Our Lord never spoke with guile. He did not shade the truth or mislead others. He did not flatter. He was sincere in all his dealings with men, from revealing their desperate need because of sin, and addressing self-righteousness, to holding out the promise of eternal life. In all his dealings he was pure. Likewise, he calls his servants to be sincere (1 Thess. 2:5) and to put away flattering lips (Ps. 12:2–3; Prov. 26:28). False teachers and divisive persons employ flattery (Rom. 16:18; Jude 16)—but not the servants of Christ.

Have you ever had the experience of talking with someone about something important but then after leaving the conversation feeling unsure that you spoke with a "good faith partner"? How did it leave you feeling afterwards? Perhaps a bit unsettled, if not anxious. When we think someone has been insincere in their interaction with us, it erodes our trust.

God intends deacons to be people who solve problems, sometimes by involving themselves in intimate matters of a person's life. Not surprisingly, then, sincerity in a deacon goes a long way in helping to calm distress and resolve issues. Even if the resolution is not what one would hope for, people receive immense help if they have been dealt with sincerely and lovingly. "The word of a deacon ought to be one of the strongest guarantees in the church. People both inside and outside the church must be able to take deacons at their words."[6]

QUESTIONS AND OBSERVATIONS

1) Does the potential deacon have a reputation for keeping his word?

Does he follow through on his commitments? The deacon should have a track record for completing assignments and tasks in keeping with his word. So ask, is the prospective deacon's word his bond?

2) Does the potential deacon speak consistently to different parties?

You want to have some measure of confidence that what the person says in one setting is what he will say in other settings. Deacons must be people who successfully fight against the fear of man. After all, deacons will be sent into troublesome situations, so they cannot be vulnerable to the faces of men or to the pressure sometimes felt in tense or uncertain circumstances.

3) Does the deacon speak the truth in love (Eph. 4:15)?

It is one thing to say the same thing consistently. But that will not be helpful if what is consistently said harms others or fails to edify them. "Let no corrupting talk come out of your mouths, but only such as is good for building up, as fits the occasion, that it may give grace to those who hear" (Eph. 4:29). The deacon should clothe all of his speech in the greatest of all virtues: love (1 Cor. 13:13; Col. 3:14).

4) Churches should look for men known to be fair brokers.

Are there men who already demonstrate an ability to stand in the gap between conflicted parties and serve the needs of both parties? Are there people generally trusted by the congregation as people who are impartial and who speak for justice? Our deacons often stand on the front line of caring for the body. Given that, we need people whose words can be trusted and who follow through on their commitments.

CONCLUSION

What advantage comes to the church if its servants cannot be trusted to speak truthfully and to keep their word? Churches become unsafe places if its leaders fail to be honest, transparent, and reliable. Sincerity may not be the final basis of truth, but there is no deep truth communicated where sincerity is lacking.

4

SOBER AND CONTENT

*Deacons likewise must be dignified, not double-tongued, not
addicted to much wine, not greedy for dishonest gain.*

1 TIMOTHY 3:8

⊕

Who wants to be waited on by a drunk person who badgers you
for bigger tips or tries to convince you to order more so that restaurant profits will go up? Having an intoxicated person fumbling
around and breathing fermented drink on you as you order is not
a pleasant dining experience. Nor is it pleasant to receive poor service because the waiter judges you by assuming you will not leave
a generous tip.

Paul instructs Timothy and us that deacons are "not addicted
to much wine, not greedy for dishonest gain." Like elders, deacons
should be sober and self-controlled. And they should not be people
who take advantage of others for their own profit and benefit.

It is interesting that the King James Version says that deacons
should not be given to "much wine," but that elders are "not given
to wine," as if old James wanted elders, but not deacons, abstinent.
Perhaps his elders drove the deacons to drink! In any case, in neither office should people be controlled and ruined by the grape.

Also, deacons must not be "greedy of filthy lucre," as the King
James Version puts it, bringing out something of the ugliness of the
disposition. The New International Version's "pursuing dishonest
gain" sounds more polite. But such a quality is nothing other than
greed for filthy lucre.

It is particularly important to avoid this quality in deacons since they will have intimate access to the lives of many people in the congregation, particularly the vulnerable ones whom they will be called upon to help. The mission of deacons, after all, is to care for the practical concerns of the body, which often involves benevolence. That's a terrible platform to give to someone who will exploit others for his or her own gain.

QUESTIONS AND OBSERVATIONS

1) Does the potential deacon drink alcohol?

If so, have you or others observed self-control in his use of alcohol, or does he exhibit weakness or sinfulness in this area? You want to know if he is capable of saying no when offered alcohol. Does he use his freedom in this area in a way that avoids causing others to stumble, being aware of newer and weaker Christians? Would you be comfortable holding the deacon out as a model for how to responsibly use or abstain from alcohol? Much good is done in the life of others when they have leaders and teachers who model the ability to live free of addictions and compulsions.

2) Does the potential deacon exhibit godly generosity and self-denial or greed in his or her personal financial matters?

Would you characterize him as a generous giver or as a hoarder of money? You are looking for people who steward their resources in keeping with the priority of the kingdom rather than the desire for gain.

3) Does the potential deacon encourage others in generosity or does he foster selfishness and financial self-concern in others?

For instance, you might consider whether he grumbles about church finances or encourages giving and unity in financial matters. You might consider whether he is willing to invest in missions and gospel ministry or if he clamors about building concerns and financial security. Deacons should not be people who invariably tend toward building bigger barns (Luke 12:15–21) but who are rich toward God in giving beyond what they and the church are able (2 Cor. 8:1–5).

4) Does the potential deacon demonstrate pastoral care and self-sacrifice when interacting with others in need?

Does the potential deacon tend to blame others for their financial straits, or does he primarily minister to them even when admonishment or rebuke is needed? A blaming and punishing spirit isn't fitting for someone whose basic task is to solve problems and help others in difficulty. With such a person, each occasion to help will be embittering and harmful to the ones who need help.

5) Is the potential deacon honest in his financial dealings?

Does he pay his bills on time? Does he report accurately on tax returns? Is the person willing to fudge a little whenever the church's business requires sacrifice or large expenditures? A deacon must be a good witness for Christ and his church, so honesty and integrity in all his dealings are essential.

6) What is the potential deacon's attitude toward wealth?

Whether a person is wealthy isn't the issue. A person can be greedy for dishonest gain while living in a hovel or a palace. Greed lives in the heart of the poor as well as the wealthy. So consider whether the potential deacon embodies the wisdom of Agur when he says, "Two things I ask of you; deny them not to me before I die: Remove far from me falsehood and lying; give me neither poverty nor riches; feed me with the food that is needful for me, lest I be full and deny you and say, 'Who is the Lord?' or lest I be poor and steal and profane the name of my God" (Prov. 30:7–9). Does the man know how to abound and how to be abased (2 Cor. 9:8; Phil. 4:11–13)? Does he hold all things loosely or with a miser's grip? A deacon who knows how to be content "in whatever situation," as Paul puts it, will be a tremendous asset in teaching and modeling that contentment for others in the body.

CONCLUSION

I recently enjoyed a wonderful meal at a rather average restaurant. The atmosphere was okay. The food was only slightly above average.

What made the meal a great dining experience was the server. She seemed to anticipate our needs and to respond with just the right solutions. We did not need to wait for or summon her, and yet she did not linger over us either. She seemed to care about our experience, and even asked about our personal well-being. She waited for our answers and replied in grace.

When we left the restaurant we felt noticed, cared for, and encouraged. We never felt as if we were a means to a tip or an inconvenience. We felt served by someone who enjoyed serving. This is how a congregation should feel as the deacons care for its needs.

5

KEEPS HOLD OF THE FAITH

They must hold the mystery of the faith with a clear conscience.
1 TIMOTHY 3:9

✛

I have an occasional ritual when visiting restaurants, especially restaurants I don't know very well. I like to have the waiter surprise me with whatever he or she thinks I will enjoy eating. The ritual started when some coworkers and I went to a restaurant following an excruciatingly long day of meetings and decision making. I simply didn't have another decision left in me.

So I handed the beautiful full-color menu of mouth-watering fare to the waitress and asked, "Could you please order something for me? I'm an omnivore, so there isn't much probability of disappointing me." After some surprise and hesitation, the waitress returned with a scrumptious meal. She spared me the agony of another decision that day, and a new personal ritual was born.

In the ten years or so that I've been doing this, I count only two instances where a waiter delivered something disappointing. Once, on a busy day like the first day this ritual developed, I told the young man I had a ravenous craving for red meat, and he brought me a large plate of shrimp and grits! Now, I know shrimp and grits is a South Carolina low-country delicacy, but there is no way to adequately refuel my tank with porridge and sea scavengers. My jaw nearly hit the table when my eyes fastened on this "meal."

To relieve my servers of too much pressure, I assure them that I will eat contentedly and gratefully whatever they bring. So when the shrimp and grits arrived, I gave thanks to the Lord and enjoyed the dish.

This entire ordering philosophy rests on one simple fact: the waiter or waitress should know the menu and the kitchen far better than I do. Their knowledge of what the chef cooks well, what customers appreciate, and what ingredients are available to make a delicious meal either makes this a great strategy or a grand adventure in culinary tomfoolery. But as I said, only twice have I worn a dunce cap during my meal. Waiters and waitresses generally know their product.

KNOWING THE FAITH

What is true for table servers in restaurants ought to be truer still for table servers in the Lord's church. Deacons must know their "product." In the words of the apostle Paul, deacons "hold the mystery of the faith with a clear conscience" (1 Tim. 3:9).

The practical "table server" aspects of deacon ministry may inadvertently obscure the utter necessity that deacons be people sound in the faith. Since deacons care for the practical needs of the body, perhaps even being assigned a specific area of service, we may run the risk of thinking of deacons as technocrats with specialized skills but little or no theological acumen. We may think of deacons as doers but not as thinkers.

But to "hold the mystery of the faith with a clear conscience" requires a steel grip on the gospel of Jesus Christ. It implies at least three requirements.

First, there is a cognitive requirement. Deacons must know and give assent to our Lord's teaching as recorded in the Holy Scripture, especially the facts concerning his life, death, and resurrection and the theological implications that follow. Deacons must understand the claims of the Bible. They must be able to articulate and explain the cardinal points of the gospel and of Christianity.

How else can deacons be the kind of servants that point others to Jesus as they serve?

Second, there is an experiential requirement. The prospective deacon needs to have embraced the faith himself. He must give witness to a personal trust or reliance upon Jesus alone for salvation. He should demonstrate genuine repentance and faith. A deacon must not be an unbeliever, unsound in the faith, or unable to give a credible profession of faith and knowledge of the gospel.

Third, the deacon must hold these truths "with a clear conscience." That is, his life and conscience must conform to the faith he professes. It's not merely that he holds the truth of the gospel without doubt or mental reserve, but he must also live a life worthy of the Christian calling (Eph. 4:1).

What are we looking for in spiritual table servers? We are looking for people who know the truth of God's Word in their own converting experience and with sufficient understanding to live and model it for others. Congregations should not neglect this qualification, because deacons inevitably find themselves in gospel conversations, applying the truth of the faith to their ministries and the lives of the people. They must keep hold of the faith.

QUESTIONS AND OBSERVATIONS
1) Does the prospective deacon give a credible profession of personal saving faith in the Lord Jesus Christ?
If the church practices some form of membership interview as part of its membership process, other leaders will likely have heard the person's testimony of conversion. But when considering someone for service as a deacon, it is a good practice to set apart time for the leaders and the congregation to hear and discuss the potential deacon's testimony. Such a time should not be an inquisition. But it gives the congregation the opportunity to affirm evidences of God's grace in a person's life.

2) Does the prospective deacon understand the gospel?
Part of the person's testimony should include a statement of the gospel itself. What has the person believed about God, man, Jesus Christ, repentance, and faith? Can he articulate and defend the biblical truth about the triune nature of God, about the creation and fall of man, the person and work of Jesus Christ, and the nature of true conversion? Mars Hill Church in Seattle, Washington, requires its leaders to answer, in writing, a series of theological questions based upon their statement of faith.

3) Is the prospective deacon given to falling away from the faith?
Can you discern any habits or patterns that suggest the prospective deacon may lose a grip on the Christian faith and life? Is the person's witness stable and strong, or do notable seasons of volatility and inconsistency exist? To keep hold of the faith a person must persevere in faith and witness.

4) Does the prospective deacon bring the truth of the gospel and the Scripture to bear on his life and ministry?
Deacons should be people known among leaders and others as people who think from the cross outward. Their perspective on service is governed by the person and work of Christ, not on other philosophies and ideas. The manner in which they now live and think gives confidence that their service would be informed by the Word of God. They are known to open the Bible with others when thinking through issues, not relying on their own understanding. And they are known to live the faith inside and outside the church.

5) Does the prospective deacon hold the deep truths of the faith without reservation?
The plethora of rival "Christianities" makes it necessary that the servant-leaders of the church be committed to the truth revealed in Scripture. Therefore you do not want a deacon who has any major doubts or disagreements with the church's statement of faith. They must be able to sign it in good conscience, indicating their complete agreement and willingness to defend it. And they should be

committed to immediately informing the elders should they find themselves out of agreement with the church's statement of faith. Deacons should also support and uphold with clear conscience the biblical distinctives of the church, such as the church's practices on baptism or its position on women in ministry and on gender roles in the family. Insofar as a position is shown to be biblical, does the prospective deacon support these positions?

6) Is the prospective deacon someone who perseveres in faith?
Deacons often enter into church difficulties and uncertainties with the goal of bringing peace, stability, order, and fruit. To do that, they must persevere in faith and in the truth of the faith, applying God's Word and patiently awaiting fruit. There may not be, and often will not be, immediate fruit from the labor. So, deacons must be people who know how to patiently abide and persevere.

CONCLUSION

In many churches, deacons serve in the teaching ministry of the church. Where men have gifts for teaching, such service is a good thing. But whether a deacon leads a Sunday school class or not, he does profess, live, and model the deep truths of the faith before the people of God. Therefore, congregations will find it necessary for the glory of God and the health of the church to find deacons mastered by the truth of God's Word and the gospel it reveals.

6

TRIED AND TRUE

And let them also be tested first; then let them serve as deacons if they prove themselves blameless.

1 TIMOTHY 3:10

⊕

In my first job after college I served as a job coach with a little non-profit that helped people with disabilities integrate into the workplace. It was a great opportunity with a great group of people.

My main task, after helping a person find a job, was to provide on-the-job coaching during the probationary employment period. This was generally a make-or-break period, and it usually became evident quickly if the job was a good fit or not.

A number of clients quit or got fired within days or even hours. The initial employment period tested the employee, the employer, and the job coach. Employees sometimes found themselves in situations too complex for their abilities. Employers sometimes felt ill-suited for supporting people with disabilities. And, well, let's just say the job coach learned to do everything from scooping poop at a kennel (several of North Carolina's finest) to washing windows for an airline to processing data at IBM to flipping burgers at a fast-food joint. The winnowing fan separated the wheat from the chaff.

TESTING SERVANTS IN THE LOCAL CHURCH

Serving in the local church not only brings joy, but from time to time it really tests the servant. Serving others tests the depth of our love, the length of our patience, the quality of our endurance, and even the permanence of our joy. Serving brings great rewards, but sometimes those rewards come gift-wrapped in trying situations. Those who lovingly serve others can end up feeling like crash dummies designed specifically to discover the heat, force, and pain tolerance of some new product.

We call deacons to a number of difficult situations that are the result of serious needs or serious sins. So novices are vulnerable to many temptations. The battle-tested make the best applicants. Perhaps this is why the apostle Paul instructs Timothy and our churches to find table servers who have been "tested first; then let them serve as deacons if they prove themselves blameless" (1 Tim. 3:10).

Deacons must be examined or put to the test. As one commentator put it, "How this is to be done is not specified. The letter itself makes the requirements public and [1 Tim.] 5:22ff. indicates that time must be given to appraise a person's life. From this we can conclude that the testing is to be a thoughtful and careful evaluation of a man's life by a congregation aware of these needed qualifications."[7] The testing most likely involves the kinds of spiritual qualifications written about in 1 Timothy 3.

QUESTIONS AND OBSERVATIONS

1) Is the prospective deacon a mature and growing Christian?
Time does not always predict maturity, but, generally speaking, recent converts are untested and unseasoned. While no magic number of years must pass before a person becomes eligible, churches must examine someone for spiritual preparedness and capability before making him a deacon. Is the fruit of the Spirit evident in his life? Is he growing into Christlikeness and contributing to the growth of others so that all may grow up into Christ (Eph. 4:11–16)?

2) Does the prospective deacon show competence in the area of service?
Looking for competence in a deacon is not the equivalent of conducting a professional headhunter search. But wisdom and experi-

ence teach churches to look for persons already skillfully serving in the area they may be asked to lead. Perhaps they have been volunteering in some related capacity. Or perhaps they have work-related experience and expertise. "This is a universal principle of Christian ministry: the way to prepare for greater service is to be diligent in some lesser service. Faithful ministry is both rewarded by God and recognized by the church."[8] Does the deacon candidate have the required skill for filling the service need of your church?

3) Is there anything that disqualifies the prospective deacon from serving?
Whether in character or competence, does the church's testing reveal serious deficiencies—whether in character or competence—that would prohibit a person's service?

4) Is the congregation supportive of the potential deacon entering the office?
The person who passes the testing should labor with the full support and commendation of the church body and its leaders. The testing affirms the person's gifting and character and endorses his ministry. It enables confidence in service.

CONCLUSION

The Lord has not established the office of deacon as an extra to the church. The office does not exist as some obsolete appendage. Rather, deacons serve the table of the Lord in order to facilitate the advance of the gospel, the health of the body, and the rejoicing of the saints. Deacons are indispensable in the Christian church. With great reason, then, Paul concludes: "For those who serve well as deacons gain a good standing for themselves and also great confidence in the faith that is in Christ Jesus" (1 Tim. 3:13). What a noble calling!

PART TWO

FINDING RELIABLE ELDERS

7

SHEEP AND SHEPHERDS: AN INTRODUCTION TO ELDERS

✠

Do you like the smell of sheep?

I don't mean the smell of lamb chops roasting in the oven. And by "sheep" I don't mean the imaginary animals conjured and counted by insomniacs. I mean the living, bleating, wooly animals roaming in green pastures.

Truthfully, I don't have much experience with sheep or sheep farms. Once during a visit to Scotland my family and I had the honor of visiting publisher William McKenzie and family on their sheep farm. What a beautiful place for tending sheep!

But pretty quickly I learned that it is not really the smell of sheep that need concern you. It is what sheep indiscriminately drop around the pasture that poses the greater threat! With vistas as breathtaking as those in the Scottish highlands, the sheep-herding novice has a tough time keeping his eyes down to watch his step. But you should. Sheep are messy and shepherds need either good work boots or careful footing!

Repeatedly the Bible describes Christians as sheep. It is not a flattering description. But it is an accurate one. Christians are messy people. Our lives are filled with brokenness, waste, trouble, and sticky situations. We are timid, and we sometimes wander. "All we like sheep have gone astray; we have turned—every one—to his own way" (Isa. 53:6). This is why we need shepherds, men who know what to do with sheep, how to care for us, lead us, and navigate our mess!

And here's the really good news: in the Bible God reveals himself as our Shepherd.[9] The Lord of the universe tends us in all our messiness, fear, weakness, and wandering. One thinks of the well-known and comforting words of Psalm 23: "The LORD is my shepherd; I shall not want." Ezekiel paints for us a compellingly beautiful prophetic picture with these words:

> For thus says the Lord GOD: Behold, I, I myself will search for my sheep and will seek them out. As a shepherd seeks out his flock when he is among his sheep that have been scattered, so will I seek out my sheep, and I will rescue them from all places where they have been scattered on a day of clouds and thick darkness. And I will bring them out from the peoples and gather them from the countries, and will bring them into their own land. And I will feed them on the mountains of Israel, by the ravines, and in all the inhabited places of the country. I will feed them with good pasture, and on the mountain heights of Israel shall be their grazing land. There they shall lie down in good grazing land, and on rich pasture they shall feed on the mountains of Israel. I myself will be the shepherd of my sheep, and I myself will make them lie down, declares the Lord GOD. I will seek the lost, and I will bring back the strayed, and I will bind up the injured, and I will strengthen the weak, and the fat and the strong I will destroy. I will feed them in justice. (Ezek. 34:11–16)

The Lord God's determination to be the shepherd of his people thunders with each repetition of "I" or "I will." That determination finds fulfillment in the Son of God, Jesus Christ, who announced, "I am the good shepherd. The good shepherd lays down his life for the sheep" (John 10:11). Then Jesus explained:

> I am the good shepherd. I know my own and my own know me, just as the Father knows me and I know the Father; and I lay down my life for the sheep. And I have other sheep that are not of this fold. I must bring them also, and they will listen to my voice. So there will be one flock, one shepherd. For this reason the Father

loves me, because I lay down my life that I may take it up again. No one takes it from me, but I lay it down of my own accord. I have authority to lay it down, and I have authority to take it up again. This charge I have received from my Father. (John 10:14–18)

All good shepherding finds its root and model in the life and love of God revealed in Jesus Christ. Ultimately, the shepherd we need is Jesus himself.

Yet, as a gift to his flock, the Chief Shepherd appoints godly men as under-shepherds to tend the flock that he purchased with his blood (Acts 20:28). We know these under-shepherds by various titles used interchangeably, including: pastors, overseers, bishops, and elders.[10] Like the Chief Shepherd, elders or pastors watch over the flock entrusted to their care (1 Pet. 5:1–3) by leading, feeding, and protecting the sheep.

Deacons and elders make up the two enduring offices of the New Testament church. While deacons serve the practical or physical needs of the church, elders serve the overall spiritual needs of the church. The two offices are not like two chambers of government—a House and Senate with more-or-less equal authority. If deacons are table servants or waiters, then elders are *maîtres de* or head chefs. Elders exercise authority or rule in the church (1 Tim. 5:17; Heb. 13:17). However, whatever authority the elders have has been delegated to them by Jesus. Further, the Scripture and Christian love set boundaries for the proper exercise of that authority.[11] As Pastor Mark Lauderbach puts it, "An elder with no Bible is an elder with no authority." Elders do not "lord it over" the sheep. As Christ's gifts to the flock, they lead and serve in order to build up the body of Christ, not to advantage themselves (Eph. 4:11–16; 1 Cor. 12:4–11).

Also, the New Testament clearly instructs churches to appoint multiple elders to shepherd the sheep (Acts 20:17, 28; Titus 1:5). The plurality of elders seems to offer several desirable benefits. Multiple elders means multiple gifted men can share the shepherding load, teach in various settings, hold one another accountable, maintain stable leadership during change, encourage one another during difficulty, and work through the wisdom-requiring messy areas of church life. In the multitude of elders there is safety and plans are established.

Finally, elders may be paid for their work—as in the case of full-time pastors (1 Tim. 5:18)—or they may be unpaid volunteers—as with many lay elders. In either case, elders receive their reward. Faithful pastors, eager to serve from a pure heart, have the confident expectation of a great reward when the Chief Shepherd appears (1 Pet. 5:4). But unfaithful shepherds and hirelings have only the fearful expectation of judgment (Ezek. 34:1–10; John 10:12–13). God the Father will not look lightly upon either the dutiful service or the neglect of sheep purchased with the blood of his Son.

So, above all, shepherds are stewards required to be faithful (1 Cor. 4:1–2). They watch for souls as those who must give account for the sheep (Heb. 13:17). As eighteenth-century pastor Lemuel Haynes wrote:

> The work of a gospel minister has a peculiar relation to the future. An approaching judgment is that to which every subject is pointing and that renders every sentiment to be inculcated vastly solemn and interesting. Ministers are accountable creatures in common with other men; and we have the unerring testimony of Scripture that "God shall bring every work into judgment, with every secret thing, whether it be good, or whether it be evil" (Eccles. 12:14). If none of our conduct is too minute to be known, we may well conclude that important affairs relating to the work and office of gospel ministers will not pass unnoticed.[12]

In the following chapters (part 2) we examine the spiritual qualifications prerequisite for serving as an elder. We do this chiefly by meditating on the qualifications for elders listed in 1 Timothy 3. In Part 3, we turn from spiritual qualifications to the elders' duties as outlined in 1 Timothy 4. I pray that these sections help congregations receive the blessing of faithful shepherds and encourage faithful shepherds in their ministry and the hope of their reward.

8

DESIRES A NOBLE TASK

If anyone aspires to the office of overseer, he desires a noble task.

1 TIMOTHY 3:1

⊕

In order to find reliable men to serve as elders, the first thing we need to look for is men who desire this "noble task." We want men who have a heart for it, who "aspire to the office."

This, in my experience, is not as straightforward as it sounds. Some men may "want the office," but their wanting is really lust for power, and so they are not fit. Conversely, some men who are fit for the office think that wanting it shows pride, ungodly ambition, or impoliteness. Finally, some men are probably qualified, but they either lack the desire or think they are not qualified because they're holding onto some idea of a "super elder."

STIRRING ASPIRATION

Practically speaking, one of the first things a pastor must do is *clarify and teach godly ambition*, including the godliness of aspiring to be an elder.[13] Faithful pastors will regularly encourage young men (including twenty-somethings) to include in their personal aspirations the goal of becoming an elder. After all, every characteristic that Paul lists for elders in 1 Timothy 3, except for the quality of being "able to teach" (v. 2), should mark every Christian man. The pastoral challenge to aspire to be an elder is good and godly. It's another way of saying to Christian men, "This is what Christian maturity and Christlikeness look like." Such maturity and Christlikeness ought to be desired, not shied away from or downplayed.

Can you imagine the Christ-exalting power of a church filled with men possessing a strong, godly desire to lead Christ's sheep in their homes and their church? In my experience, the problem in many churches falls at the other end of the spectrum—most men aspire for little more than comfort, anonymity, ease, and just about anything else except leadership responsibility.

Second, a pastor will likely have to *clarify and teach the goodness of the leadership task*. Paul calls leadership in the local church "noble." And it is. But many men may have the impression that leadership is a burden, a headache, or a necessary evil. Others may think that religious leaders are all swindlers and fakes. For a couple of years, I resisted the internal call to ministry because I did not want to be associated with television preachers and unsavory pastors caught in scandal. I remained resistant until God made the goodness of the leadership task more evident to me. So it may be necessary for current elders, without painting a false picture of unending comfort, to develop, discuss, preach, and model joy in the ministry. After all, the Lord intends leading his church to be a joy for those men with the privilege (Heb. 13:17).

WHY THE OFFICE OF ELDER IS NOBLE

Part of the nobility of the task comes from *the beauty and privilege* of modeling Christ for his people. The elder sets an example in all things (1 Tim. 4:12). He embodies in significant degree what following Jesus looks like, possesses an observable degree of the Lord's character, and provides a pattern for others to follow. The man not desiring to model Christ should be asked, "What exactly is more worthwhile than modeling Christ?"

The *necessity* of Christian leadership also makes the task noble. The Lord designed the church in such a way that it requires godly leaders. The sheep need shepherds. Without shepherds the sheep wander into all sorts of dangers and hurts, and the Savior grieves over their aimless and vulnerable condition (Matt. 9:36). Sheep tending is a good thing.

So noble is spiritual shepherding that one pastor could write, "With all my discouragements and sinful despondency; in my better moments, I can think of no other work worth doing compared with this. Had I a thousand lives, I would willingly spend them in it: and had I as many sons, I should gladly devote them to it."[14]

The task is noble and therefore to be desired. But practically, what are some things we can do or questions to ask in order to discern which men have this godly ambition?

TRAITS TO WATCH FOR

1) Take note of those men who *regularly attend the church's services and the church's business meetings.* If you have Sunday morning and evening services, they are at both. Start with those who already show an active commitment to the ministry and who model that commitment to the body. It's easier to put a man's existing desire and commitment to work than to stir up an apparent lack of desire. The pastor who rides the natural momentum of a prospective leader's desire will find it a smoother ride in comparison to the bumpy or inert carriage of a man with no active desire—even if the man evidences all the other qualities in abundance.

2) Note the men who *already appear to be shepherding members of the church even though they don't have the title "elder" or "pastor."* Specifically, who are the men that care for others by visiting or practicing hospitality, by giving counsel (often being sought after by others), and by participating in the teaching ministry of the church? You want to find the men who are eager to watch over their fellow brethren and are happy to do so without recognition. Those who naturally and quietly go about the work of loving God's people are ideal for this noble task.

3) Note those men who *show respect and trust in the existing leadership,* who work to understand the directions pursued by leadership, who ask good and appropriate questions in appro-

priate settings, and who avoid creating confusion or dissension in public meetings. A man will not lead well until he first shows himself able to submit to leadership. Should a man become one of the shepherds in a congregation, he will soon find that he needs to submit as a leader, since leadership is not reducible to always directing others.

4) Be patient and note those men who *evidence the desire over time*. Watch a man. Encourage him. Observe the desire in fruitful seasons, in dry times, when he is full of joy, and when he is sorrowful. Does the desire persist, grow, and strengthen, or does it fade, wither, and weaken? If the desire is delayed, does he wander away to do other things? You want to find men who handle delays and disappointments with maturity and humility, not impatience and immaturity. And his desire for the office itself, even if delayed, should mature over time like a fine wine. As Paul says, we do well to "not be hasty in the laying on of hands" (1 Tim. 5:22).

QUESTIONS AND OBSERVATIONS

When examining a man for the office of elder, ask him some of these questions in order to discern his desire for the office:

1) Have you ever thought of being an elder?
Start here. Many have never considered it and will be surprised that we ask. Others have considered it and may have put it out of their minds because of incorrect impressions, which we might be able to correct. For those who have not considered it, we need to be prepared to give them some reasons why they should, ranging from "this is one way of defining Christlike maturity for Christian men" to "I have seen these particular things in you that suggest to me this is something you should think about." We do not want to pressure a man, but suggesting the idea of leadership may stir a desire that causes him to think differently about where to invest his life.

2) Have you considered that your lack of desire might be an indication of spiritual complacency or misdirection?

This question assumes that desiring the office is a good thing and that the qualifications for the office are a good self-assessment for Christian maturity. Pastorally, we want to press that vision into our men. And where there is an evident lack of desire, you can assume that pastoral care, teaching, and correction may be required.

3) Why do you desire to be an elder? To what extent are you aware of anything impure (pride, power, etc.) in your motives?

This is a question, obviously, for those who are considering eldership. Because we do not want to lay hands on any man hastily, we need to practically tease out godly ambition from impure motives. No one possesses perfect motivations. We all wrestle with indwelling sin. But due diligence requires us to help a man excavate his heart and to inspect what's unearthed. Are we looking at a humble man desiring to serve, or an unsubmissive, proud seeker of control? What's the source of his eagerness and desire—service or recognition? We should avoid calling men who may desire oversight "for shameful gain" or to be "domineering over those in their charge" (1 Pet. 5:2–3). The sheep benefit immensely when we discover such attitudes *before* a man is made an elder rather than after he has beaten the sheep. What's more, confidence and assurance come to a man when he freely serves with pure motives (1 Thess. 2:3–6, 10).

4) Have you ever considered what would happen to the church, to the sheep, if they had no shepherd? Does your heart respond the same way as Jesus's at the sight of shepherdless sheep (Matt. 9:36; Mark 6:34)?

For those men who may recognize giftedness and some qualification in themselves, but who may shrink away from leadership, it may help to take the man's eyes off himself and focus them on the people he would be called to serve. More is at stake than whether an individual feels comfortable with the idea of leadership, though that should be considered. At stake is the spiritual care of the sheep.

5) Have you considered what your avoiding leadership teaches the congregation about this noble task and the care of souls?

Sometimes gifted and qualified men may already be seen as shepherds in the eyes of the body, but for some reason they are avoiding formal recognition as an elder. In such cases, we should help them to realize that they are teaching the congregation about leadership even in their avoidance. They are teaching them that even the most spiritual and gifted men in the eyes of the body think leadership is a burdensome or unnecessary task. And in teaching this through their example, men unintentionally lower the congregation's standard and expectation for its leaders, and consequently lower the quality of spiritual care they and future generations may receive. The Bible commands the congregation to "remember your leaders, those who spoke to you the word of God. Consider the outcome of their way of life, and imitate their faith" (Heb. 13:7). We do not want the Lord's people to imitate low standards and work avoidance when it comes to so noble a task.

CONCLUSION

Choosing pastors is the most important decision a congregation makes, since the pastors will shape the congregation through their teaching and their model. Given this shaping influence, the Lord calls us to find men who "shepherd the flock of God . . . exercising oversight . . . willingly, as God would have [us] . . . *eagerly* . . . being examples to the flock" (1 Pet. 5:2–3). William Still, a faithful pastor who trained men for Christian service, observed, "My whole concern in my work of trying to make pastors (and I have 'made' too few, although I have had many men through my hands) is that they become men of God; then, the pastoral work will look after itself. It will still have to be done. But the man of God is made for that."[15]

May the Lord give us discernment, patience, and clarity of observation as we seek reliable men who desire this noble task.

9

ABOVE REPROACH

If anyone aspires to the office of overseer, he desires a noble task. Therefore an overseer must be above reproach.

1 TIMOTHY 3:1–2

⊕

The nobility of the pastoral office demands a correspondingly noble character. Churches must therefore seek men whose inner and outer lives are sewn together by integrity and Christlikeness.

Paul lists "above reproach" as the second characteristic an elder must possess. "Above reproach" serves as an umbrella for all the other requirements that follow. A man must be blameless in his outward conduct, upright and just in his dealings with others.

AN OVERSEER MUST BE ABOVE REPROACH

Being above reproach means that an elder is to be the kind of man whom no one suspects of wrongdoing and immorality. People would be shocked to hear this kind of man charged with such acts. Being above reproach does *not* mean that he maintains sinless perfection. It means that his demeanor and behavior over time have garnered respect and admiration from others. He lives a life worthy of the calling of God (Eph. 4:1; 5:1–2; Phil. 1:27; Col. 1:10–12).

It's critically important for an elder to be above reproach for at least two reasons. First, everyone will assume at least two things once he is made an elder: that he is an example to all the sheep in all areas of life (1 Tim. 4:12; 1 Pet. 5:1–3); and that he will receive the benefit of the doubt against uncorroborated allegations of wrongdoing (1 Tim. 5:19). Few things are worse for a church than having a man who lacks good character be able to set a bad example while also being shielded by the generosity of judgment that comes with the office.

Second, it's critically important because an elder must be held in high esteem for his character, not for his wealth, popularity, or other worldly things. We may be tempted to grant the eldership to men on the grounds that they have made it in the business world, have a long family history with the church, or are popular and well regarded. But the apostle is not interested in any of these things. He's interesed in a dignity of character commensurate with the office. If a man is popular in the worldly sense but is not above reproach, he will likely lead out of his popularity instead of character. He may fear man more than God (a big temptation for this office), or attempt to run the church like his business, or assume certain "rights" because of his standing in the community. And all these will cripple an eldership for a time.

All Christians should be above reproach, but Christian elders *must* be. How do we find such men?

TRAITS TO WATCH FOR

1) Take note of those men who are *faithful in their dealings inside the church*. For example, do they keep their commitment to give regularly and sacrificially to the church? Do they swear to their own hurt, keeping their word even when others might not blame them for backing out of a commitment?

2) Take note of men who *command respect from others*, in the best sense of that phrase. These are the men who inspire uprightness in others. Their very presence seems to help people "straighten up" or show more zeal. People nominate this kind of man for positions requiring ethical integrity, because they are confident he will do the right thing.

3) Take note of those men who *carry on their lives outside the church with integrity*. They are men who show up at work on time.

They hold a steady job and are known for excellent work habits. They manage their financial affairs well, paying debts and living within their means. They don't fail to meet obligations.

QUESTIONS AND OBSERVATIONS

Once church leaders or the congregation have a man in mind who may be "above reproach," they might ask him a few questions.

1) Is there anything in your life that you feel disqualifies you from serving as an elder?

Although the question is very general in scope, it offers a good way to begin. It allows you to hear how the man assesses himself and possibly to find out more about his integrity. There may be issues not explicitly addressed by 1 Timothy 3 but that nonetheless trouble the prospective elder or disqualify him. This question gives the man an opportunity to raise issues that may trouble his conscience. Leaders and congregations then have an opportunity to shepherd the man through troublesome matters and model the kind of care and accountability expected of elders.

2) Would any of your coworkers or family be surprised to hear that you are a leader in your church?

Here, you are probing for whether the man's reputation is good among people outside the church. The question relies on the man's knowledge (imperfect) of his reputation among others. Church leaders may decide to ask some of the man's business associates or coworkers this question in order to gather responses from them.

3) Are there people who would say you should not serve in any church's leadership? And why would they say this?

Elders should enjoy good reputations inside and outside the church. If there is some outstanding grievance or criticism from others, it would be good to explore (a) the nature of that dispute, (b) how the potential elder has handled that issue (whether in a godly fashion or not), and (c) whether the opinion of others disqualifies the man.

CONCLUSION

The nobility of the office requires that it be held only by men with befitting integrity. In a day where most people, Christians included, are repulsed by the idea of judging others, churches must still work patiently to discern whether a man's character is mature and above reproach, even if it's one of the most difficult things churches do in finding reliable men. The health and purity of the Lord's bride requires it.

Cultivating this kind of integrity in church leaders is vital to church health.

10

A ONE-WOMAN MAN

Therefore an overseer must be above reproach, the husband of one wife.

1 TIMOTHY 3:2

⊕

Desire is the first thing Paul lists. Next comes an omnibus statement: "above reproach." And then what must those leading the Lord's church be? An elder must be "the husband of one wife," says the apostle. Literally, the phrase reads "one-woman man." Here, there are some differences of opinion as to what this means.

WHAT IS A ONE-WOMAN MAN?

There are a range of views on what Paul means by a "one-woman man," ranging from a narrow definition focused on polygamy to a broad definition focused on moral and sexual purity. Taking a narrower view, John Calvin follows Chrysostom by asserting that Paul "expressly condemns polygamy." Calvin argues that "Paul forbids polygamy in all who hold the office of a bishop, because it is a mark of an unchaste man, and of one who does not observe conjugal fidelity."[16] D. A. Carson takes this position as well.[17]

Taking the broader interpretation, John MacArthur does not understand "one woman man" to refer to marital status at all but to moral and sexual purity. "This qualification heads the list, because it is in this area that leaders are most prone to fail." MacArthur rejects the polygamy argument, saying it was "not common in Roman society and clearly forbidden by Scripture."[18]

In his excellent series of sermons on 1 Timothy, Phil Ryken takes a broad view akin to MacArthur's:

> To be above reproach, an elder must be "the husband of one wife." This does not prohibit bachelors from serving as elders. Commonly, elders will be married, and God will use the demands of their callings as husbands and fathers to do much of the sanctifying work that needs to be done in their lives before they are ready to serve as officers in the church. But remember that Paul himself was single and commended singleness to others as an opportunity for greater service in the kingdom of God (1 Cor. 7:17; 9:5). Some suggest that the phrase means "married only once." This would disqualify widowers who remarry, as well as men who have been through a divorce. If this is what Paul meant, however, one might expect him to be more explicit.
>
> The point of the phrase is probably more general: elders must be morally accountable for their sexuality. The Greeks and the Romans of the day generally tolerated gross sexual sin. Polygamy was practiced by both Greeks and Jews. Marriage was undermined by frequent divorce, widespread adultery, and rampant homosexuality. The words of Demosthenes show the scope of the problem: "Mistresses we keep for the sake of pleasure, concubines for the daily care of our persons, but wives to bear us legitimate children."[19]

Though commentators differ on the precise meaning of the phrase, everyone would agree that sexual purity is a prerequisite for holding the office of elder. Indeed, sexual purity in the church plays an important apologetic and evangelistic function in Christian witness (see, for example, Eph. 4:17–24; 5:3–14). Churches' leaders must therefore examine an elder candidate's life in this regard.

How do we find the sexually pure "one-woman man" in the congregation? Here are some questions and observations, first for single men and then for married men.

QUESTIONS AND OBSERVATIONS CONCERNING SINGLE MEN

1) How would you characterize the man's dating and fellowship with Christian women?

A man given to serial dating may be undiscerning and careless with the hearts of Christian sisters. If he is playful in matters of the heart, he may need to be discipled in this area and will not be an appropriate example to the flock. Does he treat sisters in the faith "with absolute purity" (1 Tim. 5:2 NIV)?

2) What are a man's entertainment choices? Does he view sexually explicit material or pornography?

If he is embattled with this issue, it is best not to make such a man an elder. An elder must be an example, teaching younger men to be self-controlled (Titus 2:6), and a life of sexual impurity is incongruent with the office.

3) How does the man battle lust? Does he gouge out his eye and cut off his hands (Matt. 5:27–30)?

The warfare against sexual immorality must be waged at the level of a man's heart or desire. Elders should fight their sins like Christians, which means they must radically deny an opportunity for the flesh, the world, and the Devil to excite their lusts. They must instead cultivate a deeper desire for Christ and the things of Christ. A single man who maintains camouflage in this area, who flirts with or coddles his lust, endangers himself and others. An elder must desire and accept accountability in this area.

Though the first question above would have to be reformulated, all these questions apply to married men as well. But with a single man, determining if he is a one-woman man requires thinking about the trajectory of his affections rather than his marital behavior. Do his behaviors tend toward purity, or is their evidence of immaturities, which should be avoided?

There are several further questions to consider with a married man.

QUESTIONS AND OBSERVATIONS CONCERNING MARRIED MEN

1) Does the man evidence fidelity to his wife? Is he faithful emotionally and physically?

A potential elder should be asked directly if he has ever broken the marital covenant through an adulterous relationship. And if not the physical act, has he become emotionally involved with someone in a way that disqualifies him from the office? It may be wise to have this conversation with a man's wife as well since she may provide insight into his blind spots. In general, church leaders should make sure that a woman believes that her husband is qualified for eldership. These are all questions to ask before making a man an elder, not after. The position and requirements of eldership will only add stress to any fractures already present in the marriage.

2) Does he arrange his interactions with female coworkers and women in the church allowing for full accountability and transparency?

For example, does he carefully avoid potentially compromising and tempting situations with women (traveling or meeting alone, etc.)? Elders who work in coed environments ought to be the kind of men who are trusted by female coworkers, and trusted not because they have counseled women through intimate matters but because they have appropriately avoided such intimate encounters by establishing safe distance from temptation.

3) Has the potential elder faithfully made his home marriage-centered?

By God's design, the center of the family should be the marriage of one man and one woman (Gen. 2:24). Men and women leave and cleave from their parents and become one flesh. Being a one-woman man means, in part, maintaining a family atmosphere that disallows other people or things (children and work, for example) from displacing the marriage as the center of the family. A potential elder prizes his wife even above the other precious people in the home, and in earthly relationships directs his affections first and foremost to his wife.

4) Does the prospective elder joyfully embrace the Bible's teaching on gender roles?

Does he believe in the equality of men and women while maintaining the distinct God-ordained roles for men and women in the home and in the church? An elder must teach the church how to joyfully accept all of God's instruction for life. In avoiding or abandoning God's Word on this matter, the prospective elder resists the authority of Scripture and obscures the gospel of Jesus Christ (Eph. 5:22–32). When it comes to gender roles, many men feel pressure to avoid this sensitive topic. But in doing so, they will necessarily substitute man's wisdom for God's wisdom and forfeit how God means to bless both men and women.[20]

CONCLUSION

In the culture at large, divorce rates are alarmingly high, and frequent assaults are made against marriage. That means that churches that ordain only one-woman men are holding high a gospel-centered, God-ordained alternative for the world to see. While the world plummets headlong into sexual immorality and relative ethics, the church must bear the standard for holy, good, beneficially intimate lifestyles between men and women. The elder will be at the head of this countercultural alternative. So selecting men who are faithful in these areas requires patient, prayerful discernment for the good of all.

11

SOBER-MINDED, SELF-CONTROLLED, RESPECTABLE

Therefore an overseer must be . . . sober-minded, self-controlled, respectable.

1 TIMOTHY 3:2

✠

Shopping malls are not my favorite places. I suppose I'm the stereotypical male. I storm to the one store (at most three) that potentially has what I am searching for, select the item, and then do my best to escape the whole harrowing experience through the closest exit.

Vanity Fair is such a dangerous place to be. Of all that could be said about malls, this is certainly true: they don't exist to promote sober-mindedness and self-control. Advertisements, displays, samples, music—the entire experience aims to separate people from their wallets in the most intemperate, unrestrained way possible. Sobriety is disdained. Self-control is flung off.

Over and against the materialistic seductions of the local mall, there stands the call of Scripture to Christians to be sober and self-controlled, to be good stewards, and to conquer the flesh. Not surprisingly, the apostle Paul insists that leaders in the church, elders or pastors, must be temperate and self-controlled.

The word *nephalios*, translated as "temperate" (NIV), "sober-minded" (ESV), and "vigilant" (KJV) includes the idea of being watchful or circumspect. Temperate people are free from the excessive influence of passion, lust, or emotion. The Lord calls his under-shepherds to be sober in their desires, feelings, and attitudes. The temperate man places limitations on his own freedom. He is not drunk with wine, power, lust, or anything else. He understands that not every situation is a paper bag to punch your way through.

That brings us to the next qualification, self-control. This term and the last one are closely related and aim generally at the same thing: an elder must be a person who bridles himself. He must control his internal state (emotions and so forth) and his outward actions. He is decent in conduct. He is not rash or unthinking, but sensible, discreet, and wise. Foolish actors are unfit for leadership in the Lord's church. Alexander Strauch rightly observes, "Much more damage is done to our churches by out-of-control anger than we care to admit."[21]

Where soberness and self-control reign, there you have a respectable man. He lives a godly, ordered life. Such qualifications are necessary for shepherding the flock of God.

QUESTIONS AND OBSERVATIONS

1) Does the potential elder teach other men to live as he lives?
This is the essential calling of the elder (Titus 2:2). The elder candidate should be known for encouraging sober-minded, self-controlled, respectable behavior in others. Do others learn moderation by his counsel and example?

2) Is a man trendy? Is he a lover of fads, bouncing from one new thing to another?
A trendy man places emphasis on novelty, so by definition things outside himself exert control over him. He hungers for the ever-changing, ever-elusive "next great idea." He may be "down" with the coolest in the congregation, but the very basis of that acceptance stems from the kind of instability that works against sobriety, watchfulness, and self-control.

We might see this in his style of dress or other purchases (cars, etc.). While we do not wish to be prudish about outward things, outward trendiness *might* be an early warning sign of trendiness in the more important world of ideas. Is this a man who chases every new church fad or model for doing church? Is he drawn to novel theological ideas? Trendiness has nearly destroyed the church from within, and such things should be avoided. Instead, we should look for men who are steadfast in their resistance to fads and unhealthy trends and who adopt a consistently sound, biblical view of themselves, the world, and God. We are looking for classic, well-worn suits rather than the latest Paris avant-garde couture.

3) Are the man's appetites balanced? Is there any place where he is given to excess—food, alcohol, anger?
Does the man restrain himself, exercising control and demonstrating contentment in all things? Men addicted to alcohol, drugs, sex, or other things are not suitable candidates for the office of elder.

4) We should take note of the man's actions and reactions in various situations.
How does he behave when things are going well? Is he self-controlled, praising the Lord, but not abusing his prosperity? What are his demeanor and conduct like when circumstances turn tough? Does he handle suffering in a composed way? Does he persevere in adversity, not overcome by fear, resentment, or cowardice? Is the man a complainer? A complainer may be a man imbalanced in his desires, assuming that things should be done his way or at least a different way.

5) Do others respect how this man lives his life?
Are his enemies unable to condemn him and ashamed in the face of his life and witness (Titus 2:7–8)?

CONCLUSION

The ministry and the church are always being watched by people inside and outside, and the church's enemies continually look for opportunities to condemn it and slander it. Churches are greatly helped to withstand this onslaught when its leaders are respectable in their conduct and are men of sound judgment.

12

HOSPITABLE

Therefore an overseer must be . . . hospitable.
1 TIMOTHY 3:2

✠

On my first Sunday morning visiting Capitol Hill Baptist Church in Washington, DC, my family and I sat in front of a lovely family in the church balcony. I first noticed them because their young children sat attentively and patiently as they participated in the service. I then noticed their lovely, vigorous singing. But they really grabbed my attention when they greeted us warmly immediately after the service. The man of the family took me around and introduced me to many of the men in the church, and after about fifteen minutes or so invited my family to join his family at their home for lunch—right then.

Honestly, the experience made me feel a little weirded out. First of all, his name was Jim, and literally the first three men he introduced me to were all named Jim. *Strange,* I thought. *What kind of church is this? Will I have to change my name again?* Then the quick invitation to lunch about knocked me down. It happened too fast. And with my Southern upbringing, it might have even been considered impolite.

So I gave him my best polite Southern way of saying no: "That is mighty nice of you. Perhaps some other time." Everybody down South knows that a sentence like that means no. Southerners know that that is how you must say no because saying no itself is impolite. Southerners are nothing if not polite.

So I had clearly said no to this man's kind but hasty offer of lunch. And wouldn't you know it? The very next week, when we went to this strange church again, he insisted that we join them for lunch. I was North Carolina. He was New Jersey. There was a failure to communicate. He didn't understand the rules of the South, but Washington, DC, apparently was too close to the Mason-Dixon Line to clearly establish which "Rome" we were in and what we should do.

But I was wrong, and Jim was right. He was the godlier man. He was more hospitable than anyone I had ever met and remains more hospitable than I am today. He embodied Paul's insistence that hospitable men lead Christ's church. And rightly, he was a church elder.

WHY SHOULD CHRISTIANS PRIZE HOSPITALITY?

First, hospitality tangibly expresses love. God calls Christians to love one another (John 13:34–35) and their enemies (Matt. 5:43–47). Hospitality gives practical form to that love. Elders should model this.

Second, hospitality tangibly expresses care for strangers. How do we know that we are caring for the strangers in our gate (Lev. 19:33–34)? One measure might be how close we get to them and allow them to get to us. Hospitality brings us close in a meaningful way. It establishes intimacy in relationships and reflects the love of Christ to the "alien."

Third, hospitality enables evangelism. Perhaps our failure to be hospitable explains why so many Christians have few non-Christian friends and find themselves far removed from evangelistic opportunities. We cannot share the gospel with a person we fail to greet, or speak to a person with whom we refuse to spend time. Apart from being hospitable on some level, sharing the good news becomes close to impossible.

Fourth, hospitality enables discipleship and fellowship. The early church devoted itself to breaking bread and fellowship (Acts 2:42–47). For those early believers, such hospitality ranked right up there with devotion to the apostles' doctrine.

So, hospitality and the modeling of hospitality are essential to the Christian life (Rom. 12:13). As one author noted, "Hardly anything is more characteristic of Christian love than hospitality. Through the ministry of hospitality we share the things we value most: family, home, financial resources, food, privacy, and time. In other words, we share our lives."[22] Churches should be filled with people given to this particular act of love (1 Pet. 4:8–9). And the church's leaders should be examples of hospitality for all.

How do we find men who are hospitable? How do we assess this qualification?

QUESTIONS AND OBSERVATIONS

1) Note those men who seem to make a ministry of greeting everyone at church.

Are they wall flowers, or are they candidates for Mr. Congeniality? This doesn't mean that a man must have a bubbly personality. But it does pay to take note of the men who hang around after church services end, who arrive early, who greet visitors and saints alike. This greeting and welcoming activity is essential to being hospitable. Note especially if a man is doing this contrary to his natural tendency. If he is, that's a sign of gospel grace. Churches should value the positive act of love that resists the natural inclination toward seclusion and privacy.

2) Note the men who help those in need.

Hospitality often extends a helping hand. Which men help seniors make their way to church? Do they give rides to other church members or visitors? Do they help to escort visitors to Sunday school classes or to the children's ministry? Hospitality means serving those in need.

3) Does the man open his home to others?

This is perhaps the most obvious form of hospitality. Identify those men who make their home a place of ministry. Perhaps they host a small-group Bible study. Perhaps they volunteer first to host a missionary or to prepare meals for visiting preachers. Maybe they often invite people over for dinner, like my friend Jim (the *first* Jim). Men with an active hospitality ministry are gems, and by their hospitality they give themselves the opportunity to intimately know and oversee the sheep.

4) Homes are not the only place to show hospitality.

A hospitable man will use a variety of times and places to show hospitality, such as the lunch hour at work. So ask, how does he use his lunch hour? Does he use it to build relationships with non-Christian coworkers with the hope of gospel opportunity? Does he meet regularly with other men in the church to build fellowship and accountability and to disciple?

5) Does he accept invitations to hospitality?

Often, receiving love and care leaves people feeling uncomfortable. The potential elder should model both the giving and the receiving of love. It is especially important that he spend time with different kinds of people in the congregation (young, old, wealthy, poor, different ethnicities, etc.). Many people want to feel strong and without any need for others' care and attention. But the hospitable person honors others by accepting their hospitality with genuine thankfulness and with as little self-awareness as possible.

CONCLUSION

At the last church evening service before Jim and his family were relocated from Washington, DC, the pastor asked everyone who had been guests in their home for lunch or dinner to stand. In the service that night were probably 350 to 400 people. Literally 90 percent of the congregation stood and gave God praise for the hospitality of Jim's family. Their home and their lives had become a very real extension of the church's ministry and pastoral care. They bore immeasurable fruit simply by having people join their normal Sunday dinner, week after week.

If that sounds like a burden, I should also mention that Jim and his wife have six children as well as their adopted nephew and niece, and they lived forty-five minutes from the church. He was not Superman, but the way he and his family modeled hospitality sometimes made it seem like he was. His example challenges me to forsake ease and to cross more boundaries with the love of Christ. May Jim's tribe increase!

13

ABLE TO TEACH

Therefore an overseer must be . . . able to teach.

1 TIMOTHY 3:2

✤

Have you ever noticed in the New Testament how significant the activity of teaching is? Pastors think about the importance of teaching all the time, since it relates to their job. But it's worth noting that in the New Testament, teaching appears to be necessary to every aspect of the Christian's life.

We call ourselves "disciples" and we practice spiritual "disciplines," words whose roots have to do with teaching and learning. So teaching is a central part of proclaiming the gospel and making disciples: ". . . teaching them to observe all that I have commanded you" (Matt. 28:19–20). Teaching is critical for training younger generations of men and women (Titus 2:2–6). Teaching is necessary for people to learn how to pray (Luke 11:1). Indeed, teaching is right at the heart of Christian maturity (Eph. 4:11–16). The Bible even connects singing with teaching, since in singing we speak and admonish one another in song (Eph. 5:19; Col. 3:16).

We could go on. Teaching and the necessity of teaching appear everywhere on the pages of the New Testament. Even in the Old Testament, teaching the word of God played a dominant role in reviving and strengthening God's people in faithfulness.

THE NECESSITY OF TEACHING

So when the apostle Paul includes "able to teach" in his list of qualifications for church leadership, we should not be surprised.

Every other attribute listed by Paul should typify *every* maturing Christian man, but the quality "able to teach" is the one peculiar gift required for men who would be elders or pastors. The reason is simple: teaching is the primary task of the elder. Other things are necessary in a church, such as administration, mutual care, and so forth. But the one thing that necessarily sets an elder apart is his ability to teach.

John Calvin captures something of the sobriety needed when approaching this task:

> And if it be deemed a great wickedness to contaminate any thing that is dedicated to God, he surely cannot be endured, who, with impure, or even with unprepared hands, will handle that very thing, which of all things is the most sacred on earth. It is therefore an audacity, closely allied to a sacrilege, rashly to turn Scripture in any way we please, and to indulge our fancies as in sport; which has been done—by many in former times.[23]

WHAT DOES THE APOSTLE MEAN BY "ABLE TO TEACH"?

Paul's criterion "able to teach" refers to the ability to communicate and apply the truth of Scripture with clarity, coherence, and fruitfulness. Those who have this ability handle the Scripture with fidelity, and others are edified when they do. This ability is not limited to public teaching from the pulpit. Men with this ability might be gifted public teachers, or they might simply be gifted for one-on-one or small-group settings. Some men are not exceptional public speakers, but they are teaching and counseling the people around them from the Scriptures all the time. Such men should not be disqualified from the office of elder.

Earlier I told you the story about Mark Dever, who on hearing my desire to pastor immediately asked my wife, "Can he teach?" It was the first question he asked. Teaching ability is the unique gift associated with the office of elder, and aspiring men must possess it. We must not overlook this qualification when assessing a candidate for pastoral leadership: Can he teach?

QUESTIONS AND OBSERVATIONS

1) Pastors must look for ways to provide men in the church opportunities to teach in order to assess giftedness and ability.

Men who have an interest in teaching and who meet biblical qualifications for the office of elder should be given opportunities to teach in appropriate settings. Some churches use their Sunday evening services to this end. Other churches use Sunday school opportunities or mid-week Bible studies. Still others organize teacher training and workshop experiences. Whatever the local situation, pastors and churches should create opportunity to observe and affirm the teaching gifts of men in the congregation.

2) Assuming a man has had a number of opportunities to teach, how capable is he?

Pastors should probably grant a man several opportunities to grow and learn as a teacher. His ability need not be judged on a maiden voyage. But over time, it needs to be asked whether the man demonstrates skill in interpreting a text, outlining a sermon, communicating biblical ideas clearly, applying the Scripture appropriately, and anticipating objections and pastoral needs in the body. Since teaching is central, those assessing the man should not be too hasty. It may be that a man will develop this ability over time. I had the privilege of serving with two faithful elders who were not good public speakers. One stuttered and the other nervously perspired. But in time, they became two of the best Sunday evening preachers at our church. Cultivating and assessing this gift requires clear, honest, and patient appraisal.

3) Does the man show pastoral sensibility in his teaching?

Congregations should look for men who know the body and are able to apply God's Word to God's people. Does the prospective elder show discernment in this regard? Is he able to speak to hurts, pains, joys, needs, history, and hopes in the congregation? Does he tend to beat the sheep or feed the sheep? If he knows the people, it should show up in how he nurtures them in the teaching. The apostle Paul modeled this himself, saying, "For you know how, like a father with his children, we exhorted each one of you and encouraged you and charged you to walk in a manner worthy of God, who calls you into his own kingdom and glory" (1 Thess. 2:11–12). Elders should show some of this same parental affection as they teach the people of God.

4) Is the prospective elder committed to exposition (or the church's preaching philosophy)?
Does he agree with the current elder(s) on what preaching is and should be? Does he support the teaching philosophy and approach of the church? Does he think that teaching is central to the work of the church, or does he believe something else should hold the pole position? Widely divergent views about this essential task may cause serious strain on the eldership and on the main preaching pastor as he endeavors to discharge his duty faithfully. Divergent opinions may also affect the sheep as teachers employ fundamentally different strategies in the pulpit. The elders set the character and the tone of the teaching ministry, so unity in teaching philosophy is necessary.

5) Are others edified by his teaching?
Will the congregation, if asked, affirm that this man has teaching ability and that they spiritually benefit from his teaching? Ask around to see how others receive and use a prospective elder's teaching. We can sometimes affirm or rule out a man's ability by considering how others assess him.

6) Does the man disciple others?
Since not all (or even most) teaching is public, we should look to those smaller, less public areas as well. Does the prospective elder help others grow in Christ in more private settings such as small groups or one-on-one discipleship? Is he faithful to help others work through difficulties or questions? Do others come to him

for advice and counsel? And is his counsel consistently and thoroughly biblical? A man may do a great deal of pastoral work in the hallways or in the parking lot after church or over a cup of coffee during the week. Who are those men who teach in this way?

7) Is the man theologically mature and supportive of the church's theological distinctives?

A man may have a gift, but the gift must be informed by appropriate content. Many are skilled at emotionally rousing the crowd but cannot explain the basic doctrines of the faith. So leaders and churches must assess a man's theological maturity and knowledge.

When considering a prospective elder, we should discuss the church's statement of faith in detail. Are there any points with which he disagrees? Can he sign the statement in its entirety with good conscience? His teaching should be expected to uphold that statement. Does he understand and support the theological distinctives of the church, such as the church's view of the ordinances, gender roles in the home and church, and so on? For the unity of the church, a man with teaching authority should be able to fully champion the church's distinctives.

Martyn Lloyd-Jones helpfully points to what churches should look for in a preacher or handler of the Scriptures:

> What do you look for? [T]hey should be men "filled with the Spirit." That is the first and greatest qualification. You are entitled to look for an unusual degree of spirituality, and this must come first because of the nature of the task. In addition, you are entitled to look for a degree of assurance with respect to his knowledge of the Truth and his relationship to it. It is surely clear that if he is a man who is always struggling with problems and difficulties and perplexities himself, and trying to discover the truth, or if he is so uncertain that he is always influenced by the last book he reads, and is "carried about by every wind of doctrine" and every new theological fashion, it is clear that he is *ipso facto* a man who is not called to the ministry. A man who has great problems himself and is in a state of perplexity is clearly not one who is fitted to be a preacher, because he will be preach-

ing to people with problems and his primary function is to help them to deal with them. "How can the blind lead the blind?" is our Lord's own question in such a situation. The preacher then must be a man who is characterised by spirituality in an unusual degree, and a man who has arrived at a settled assured knowledge and understanding of the Truth, and feels that he is able to preach it to others.[24]

8) Can the prospective elder defend the faith?

The ability to defend the truth is another aspect of sound teaching ability. "He must hold firm to the trustworthy word as taught, so that he may be able to give instruction in sound doctrine and also to rebuke those who contradict it" (Titus 1:9). Pastors and churches should consider whether the potential elder demonstrates an ability to correct error and preserve the truth, without being argumentative and unkind, but patiently and gently.

9) Is the man himself teachable?

Will the elder candidate be a model to the congregation as someone who humbly and joyfully receives the Word with profit? Being teachable is itself teaching; it models humility before others. If a pastor is not given to learning and submitting to the teaching of his fellow elders, he creates tension inside the eldership and may model hardness of heart before the sheep. Or worse, he may be less the teacher and more the dictator in interacting with the sheep.

CONCLUSION

As pastors and churches, we must find reliable men and entrust to them the things we have learned from faithful men. In order for the transmission of the truth to happen well, the men we appoint to leadership must be able to teach in various settings and ways. Calling a man who cannot teach, to serve as an elder, is like channeling the pure, wholesome milk of the gospel through rusty, corroded pipes. The Word continues to be milk, but for how long? And who wants to drink milk from a rusty pipe?

14

SOBER, GENTLE, PEACEMAKING

. . . not a drunkard, not violent but gentle, not quarrelsome.
1 TIMOTHY 3:3

✛

My grandfather and my brothers were alcoholics. My grandfather drank in binges. For months he remained sober, only to later "fall off the wagon," exploding in verbally abusive fits and sometimes violent behavior. In his sober periods, he professed to be a Christian. But when intoxicated, you could not reason with him from the Scripture or speak to him of Christ. In his later years, in declining health, he gave up drinking and became one of my favorite people. His jolly laugh caused his shoulders to jiggle and his head to fall back. And when something was particularly sweet to him, he let out a warm and oozy, "Yeeesss, Lord."

My brothers also binged. Their drinking sprees tended to be longer than my grandfather's. And like my grandfather, they lost social skill when drinking. They lost jobs. They lost friends. They also lost their families.

You will not be surprised, then, to learn that I do not have any objections to the apostle Paul's instruction in 1 Timothy 3:3: an elder or pastor should "not [be] given to drunkenness, not violent but gentle, not quarrelsome" (NIV). Drunkenness, violence, and quarreling are probably clumped together in Paul's list because they are often clumped together in life. Where you find one, you often find the others.

Though I love my grandfather and my brothers, they would not be suitable candidates for leadership in the church.

THE QUALIFICATIONS

Verses 2 and 3 of 1 Timothy 3 belong together like a color photo and its negative. In verse 2 Paul lists positive qualities: temperate, self-controlled, and respectable. In verse 3 he rules out three negative characteristics: drunkenness, violent, and quarrelsome. The qualities of verse 2, when present, qualify a man for the office. The qualities of verse 3, when present, disqualify him.

"Given to drunkenness" is as it sounds. It's a tendency to drink intoxicating beverages to excess, until losing the faculty of a sober mind. Calvin notes that drunkennes includes "any intemperance in guzzling wine."[25] An elder is not a winebibber.

Violence often follows intoxication. A brawling and violent disposition does not suit a pastor. He must not to be a "striker." Instead, gentleness controls his way. Finally, an elder must not be quarrelsome. He is not argumentative and divisive. Paul wrote the same instruction in his second letter to Timothy:

> Don't have anything to do with foolish and stupid arguments, because you know they produce quarrels. And the Lord's servant must not quarrel; instead, he must be kind to everyone, able to teach, not resentful. Those who oppose him he must gently instruct, in the hope that God will grant them repentance leading them to a knowledge of the truth, and that they will come to their senses and escape from the trap of the devil, who has taken them captive. (2 Tim. 2:23–26 NIV)

Far from being quarrelsome, the pastor avoids arguments, patiently instructs, and recognizes disputes in the church as symptoms of deeper spiritual desires (James 4:1–3). Patience, gentleness, and teaching are the rule of the day. Teaching must not be confused with lampooning every person who has a different opinion. How often have pastors found themselves enmeshed in controversy over wild and silly ideas? The church needs men who are able to see through such demonic ploys and give the people a model of soberness and peace.

QUESTIONS AND OBSERVATIONS

1) Is the elder given to drunkenness?

Does he partake of alcohol at all, and, if so, is it with appropriate sobriety? Whether at home or in the community, does he ever drink to the point of intoxication? Are there intoxicants other than alcohol that enslave him?

2) Look for men who show an ability to biblically discern between the cardinal matters of the faith and "foolish, ignorant controversies" (2 Tim. 2:23).

We may see this in a man's teaching, if he is given opportunity to share. Does he use public airtime to introduce people to doubtful opinions or speculative and fanciful ideas (Rom. 14:1)? Or does he demonstrate sound and mature judgment that emphasizes the truth of God? Is everything a matter of conscience for him—a hill to die on—or can he parse out less important and unimportant issues? Does that ability show up in his conversation with the sheep, or does he attempt to force people into the "correct" mold on every issue, no matter its significance?

3) In the midst of conflict is he patient and gentle?

Sometimes conflict in a church is the pressure that refines diamonds. Perhaps there have been difficult situations in the church's recent past or in its current life. Who demonstrates a 2 Timothy 2:24 ability to avoid foolish disputes? Who responds with gentleness and avoids retaliation and striking at "opponents"? Can you identify men who face attacks and arguments while maintaining hope that God would grant the grace of repentance to those in error? Those men maintain an eternal and spiritual perspective instead of giving in to arguments and fights.

4) Beyond avoiding fights, is the prospective candidate a peacemaker?

Does he do everything within his power to maintain unity in the church (Rom. 15:5–6; Eph. 4:3; Col. 3:15)? Conflict avoidance may be merely that—avoidance. But an agent of peace and reconciliation is something more, and an elder must be one. Peacemaking is a ministry given to all Christians, but an elder must set an example of positive peacemaking and unity building.[26] It is one thing to stay out of something, and quite another to teach others, with patience and gentleness, to lay down their arms and join arms. Such would be an excellent elder.

5) Is the man a physical abuser of his wife, his children, or anyone else?

He must not be a "striker." If the discipline of his children includes physical correction, does anger, rage, jealousy, or disappointment fuel the discipline? Or would his wife and children say that he offers sober, appropriate, and godward discipline? Is there a past history of spousal abuse? Current pastors would be wise to investigate any history of abuse, whether old or recent, whether before or after conversion to faith in Christ, and to determine if there have been well-established patterns of repentance and accountability. A man given to violence in his home obviously does not manage his own family well.

CONCLUSION

The apostle Paul anticipated seasons of increasing difficulty in the gospel ministry. "For the time is coming when people will not endure sound teaching, but having itching ears they will accumulate for themselves teachers to suit their own passions, and will turn away from listening to the truth and wander off into myths" (2 Tim. 4:3–4). For such a time as that, the apostle called for sober, gentle, and peacemaking shepherds. "As for you, always be sober-minded, endure suffering, do the work of an evangelist, fulfill your ministry" (2 Tim. 4:5). Men of this caliber bless any church.

15

NOT A LOVER OF MONEY

Therefore an overseer must be above reproach, the husband of one wife, sober-minded, self-controlled, respectable, hospitable, able to teach, not a drunkard, not violent but gentle, not quarrelsome, not a lover of money.

1 TIMOTHY 3:2–3

Paul's instructions to Timothy for finding qualified overseers reminds me of a classic O'Jays song called "For the Love of Money." Here are some of the lyrics for the uninitiated:

For the love of money
People will steal from their mother
For the love of money
People will rob their own brother
For the love of money
People cannot even walk the street
Because they never know who in the world they are gonna beat
For that lean, mean, mean green
Almighty dollar, money

For the love of money
People will lie, Lord, they will cheat
For the love of money
People do not care who they hurt or beat
For the love of money
A woman will sell her precious body
For a small piece of paper it carries a lot of weight
Call it lean, mean, mean green
Almighty dollar

Perhaps one of the most frequent criticisms made of pastors or churches is, "All they want is money." And let's be honest: with the nonstop jingles and pithy promises of payoff that fill the air on some television stations, one can understand how people might fear this. The Daddy Graces, Kenneth Copelands, and Creflo Dollars of the world have made this a real issue. And long before the contemporary televangelists stepped onto the scene, popes and their underlings sold indulgences to finance their tastes in high-quality art and soaring cathedrals.

Against all of this, the apostle Paul instructs Timothy to find men who are not lovers of money, or, as the King James Version renders it, "greedy of filthy lucre." And this latter rendering gets closer to the compound word Paul uses. Paul has in view indecent, dishonorable gain, gain even at the expense of moral character. Interestingly, the New Testament uses the term only in 1 Timothy 3:3, 8, and Titus 1:7, where Paul describes qualifications for elders and deacons. It would seem the Lord has a unique concern for an elder's attitude toward money, that he *not* be the kind of man that would sell his soul for a buck or fleece the flock for a farthing. The potential elder must renounce greed and love for money.

JOHN WESLEY'S EXAMPLE

In this day of megachurch superstars and Christian celebrities boasting multi-million-dollar estates and fortunes, churches desperately need countercultural examples. Most people assume that their lifestyle should match their income, and that their income should be ever increasing so that their lifestyle could be ever expanding. But John Wesley (1703–1791) thought otherwise. He lived such a compellingly modest life that his pattern should be studied by every prospective elder.

Charles White recounts an incident that shaped Wesley's attitude toward and approach to money.

[Wesley] had just finished buying some pictures for his room when one of the chambermaids came to his door. It was a winter day and he noticed that she had only a thin linen gown to wear for protection against the cold. He reached into his pocket to give her some money for a coat, and found he had little left. It struck him that the Lord was not pleased with how he had spent his money. He asked himself: "Will thy Master say, 'Well done, good and faithful steward?' Thou has adorned thy walls with the money that might have screened this poor creature from the cold! O justice! O mercy! Are not these pictures the blood of this poor maid?"

Perhaps as a result of this incident, in 1731 Wesley began to limit his expenses so he would have more money to give to the poor. He records that one year his income was £30, and his living expenses £28, so he had £2 to give away. The next year, his income doubled, but he still lived on £28 and gave £32 away. In the third year, his income jumped to £90; again he lived on £28, and gave £62 to the poor.

Wesley preached that Christians should not merely tithe, but give away all extra income once the family and creditors were taken care of. He believed that with increasing income, the Christian's standard of giving should increase, not his standard of living. He began this practice at Oxford and he continued it throughout his life. Even when his income rose into the thousands of pounds, he lived simply and quickly gave his surplus money away. One year his income was slightly over £1,400; he gave away all save £30. He was afraid of laying up treasures on earth, so the money went out in charity as quickly as it came in. He reports that he never had as much as £100 at one time.

When he died in 1791, the only money mentioned in his will was the miscellaneous coins to be found in his pockets and dresser drawers. Most of the £30,000 he had earned in his lifetime he had given away. As Wesley said, "I cannot help leaving my books behind me whenever God calls me hence; but, in every other respect, my own hands will be my executors."[27]

Randy Alcorn points out that Wesley's income in today's dollars would be $160,000 annually. Yet he lived on only $20,000 of it. We may not all live as radically generous a life as Wesley. However, an elder's attitude toward money and possessions should tend toward Wesley's lifestyle rather than toward the opulent life-styles of so many prosperity preachers.

QUESTIONS AND OBSERVATIONS

1) Does the prospective elder give generously and sacrificially?
Giving is one mark of freedom from the love of money and financial gain. We are to store up for ourselves treasure in heaven, not on earth, to serve the Lord and not money (Matt. 6:19–24). Prizing Christ and the things of his kingdom results in sacrificial, generous, and cheerful giving. When considering a man for elder, we should consider whether he gives generously to the work of the church (which may also be a measure of his commitment to the church). Does he give to the needs of others as opportunity permits? Or is he a hoarder?

2) Are his investments earthly minded or heavenly minded?
Surely a man must provide for the needs of his household (1 Tim. 5:8). But do his investments tend toward excess and a love for excess? Is he financially overextended? What kind of debt does he carry (consumer debts or necessary debts like mortgages)? Does he purchase fancy cars when a more modest model is an option? Does he love large and expensive houses when a more modest home might meet his needs? Is his savings disproportionate to his giving? Beyond questions of cars and houses, does he respond like the rich young ruler at the suggestion of giving it all to the poor and following Christ? In talking about these things, can the current leadership discern whether a prospective elder's heart is attached to the world? Or is there evidence of excellence in the grace of giving (2 Cor. 8:7)?

3) What is the man's philosophy about gain in this life?
What is his measure of success? Much of secular Western thought concludes, "Get all you can, can all you get, then sit on your can." Or maybe you've heard the more mercenary version of the Golden Rule: "He who has the most gold rules." Does the prospective elder

hold either of these outlooks? Is amassing money his measure of success? Is his self-worth built upon possessions and wealth? Contrast all of that with Paul's instructions to Timothy just a little later in the letter: "There is great gain in godliness with contentment, for we brought nothing into the world, and we cannot take anything out of the world. But if we have food and clothing, with these we will be content" (6:6–8). The maxim attributed to John Wesley would also be an appropriate attitude in an elder: "Make as much as you can, save as much as you can, and give as much as you can."

4) Consider the man's professional and personal decisions, whether they are calculated to pursue gain.
Does the prospective elder organize his life around the goal of monetary gain or the pursuit of kingdom objectives? "Those who desire to be rich fall into temptation, into a snare, into many senseless and harmful desires that plunge people into ruin and destruction. For the love of money is a root of all kinds of evils. It is through this craving that some have wandered away from the faith and pierced themselves with many pangs" (1 Tim. 6:9–10). The love of money will be manifested in practical decisions and schemes, leading to temptation, ruin, and destruction. Is the man given to over-work in the pursuit of gain, while his family or spiritual life suffers? Is he willing to bend the Lord's Word or commands in order to justify pursuing riches? Will he make professional and family decisions (such as accepting a promotion or moving to another area of town) to pursue gain at the expense of faithful involvement in the church, or has he denied certain opportunities in order to make spiritual objectives a priority?

5) What is his attitude toward church finances?
There are ways that a love for money affects a man's outlook on a church's financial dealings. Perhaps he will want the church to stockpile cash. He might think primarily about location in terms of real estate value instead of whether it facilitates an effective

witness. He might argue against increases in the church budget because he would rather horde than invest in solid ministry. In general, it's worth considering a man's approach to the church budget. Does he approach it with faith or with reliance on worldly wisdom? Does he rely only on what is seen, or does he call upon God and trust God's people to give beyond themselves (2 Cor. 8:1–5)? "For you know the grace of our Lord Jesus Christ, that though he was rich, yet for your sake he became poor, so that you by his poverty might become rich" (2 Cor. 8:9).

6) Does the prospective elder show more regard for money than for people?

If he had to make a decision between serving people (even at great cost) and protecting the church financially, which would he choose? Is he the kind of man who would rather be broke and serve the poor or be wealthy while surrounded by the hungry?

CONCLUSION

For a long time I resisted the urge to gospel ministry because I didn't want to be associated in any way with the hucksters who show up on television. I thought, *Lord, let me be anything but a preacher. Too many of them seem concerned only about money.* Well, the Lord will have his way, and apparently a good laugh, too. I now serve as a pastor in one of the largest banking sectors in the world with the temptations of worldliness all around! The O'Jays remind me to pray as they warn in the chorus:

> Do not let, do not let, do not let money rule you
> For the love of money
> Money can change people sometimes
> Do not let, do not let, do not let money fool you
> Money can fool people sometimes
> People! Do not let money, do not let money change you

The good news is that the Lord gives us greater loves than money, which makes wings and flies away (Prov. 23:5). He gives us greater delights in Christ, who in fact is the greatest delight of all. What a privilege it is, by God's rich grace, to preach Christ the Lamb to a world overrun with love for money. May the Lord make us all faithful and keep us from greed. And may he give to his churches men who disdain the world's trinkets and serve the Master rather than mammon.

16

LEADER AT HOME

He must manage his own household well, with all dignity keeping his children submissive, for if someone does not know how to manage his own household, how will he care for God's church?

1 TIMOTHY 3:4–5

☩

The church is a family, a group of brothers and sisters in Christ, submitted to God the Father by the working of God the Holy Spirit.

Every family requires leadership, including the church family. So the apostle Paul under the inspiration of the Holy Spirit adds another qualification for those who desire to be overseers in the Lord's family. He writes: "He must manage his own household well, with all dignity keeping his children submissive, for if someone does not know how to manage his own household, how will he care for God's church?" (1 Tim. 3:4–5).

Notice the urgency and insistence about these qualifications. Paul insists that an elder should have all the qualities that we have discussed, but here a stronger passion infuses the words. The prospective elder *must* possess these qualities. A man cannot be a qualified elder if he does not consistently manage his household well. It's a prerequisite. It is not something he can learn on the job, but a minimum qualification for even accepting the application. If he cannot manage this smaller household, he cannot manage God's larger household, the church. God calls an elder to nothing less than tending to God's family and household.

Women receive an unfair rap, sometimes being stereotyped as busybodies and meddlers in the affairs of others. But here Paul warns against men who could be too preoccupied with the affairs of the church and too little occupied with what's going on under their own roof. One thinks of Eli's hasty and mistaken rebuke of Hannah as she prayed, while simultaneously abdicating responsibility for his wayward boys (1 Samuel 1–2). An elder tends to affairs at home.

LEADERSHIP AND LOVE

The word "manage" in verse 5 is the same word used of the good Samaritan who risked himself to bandage and care for a wounded traveler (Luke 10:25–37). The Samaritan responded to the traveler's hurt with caring supervision and concern—precisely what the prospective elder will be called to do in the church. Elders supervise as well as nurture the family members.[28]

If a man supervises but fails to nurture, it's possible that he's either a tyrant or an absentee landlord. Neither is fitting for a father, much less an elder. If he only nurtures but fails to supervise, he's like the permissive good cop or friend to the children—he won't give appropriate guidance. He must govern the home with gentleness and concern for each member of the family. The apostle and his companions struck this balance as they handled the churches. Paul could write:

> We were gentle among you, like a nursing mother taking care of her own children. So, being affectionately desirous of you, we were ready to share with you not only the gospel of God but also our own selves, because you had become very dear to us. . . . For you know how, like a father with his children, we exhorted each one of you and encouraged you and charged you to walk in a manner worthy of God, who calls you into his own kingdom and glory. (1 Thess. 2:7–8, 11–12)

The apostle tells us immediately what good management entails—"with all dignity keeping his children submissive" (v. 4).

Paul has already addressed the fact that the prospective elder must be a one-woman man, indicating the singleness of heart a married elder must have for his wife. But here Paul concerns himself with a father's relationship with his children. The word "dignity" can apply either to the father or to the children in their submission and obedience. Of course, one expects both with a qualified elder. Such a man deserves respect, and it shows in how his children follow his leadership. He is dignified, respectful, or reverent. His children reciprocate with respect and reverence. The NIV renders this verse, "See that his children obey him with proper respect."

QUESTIONS AND OBSERVATIONS

1) Is the prospective elder attentive to his home?

Does he provide leadership there? What does his wife say about his involvement? Does she commend him or tend to rationalize away his lack of involvement in the home? Supervising the home can be measured in a number of ways, from knowing and attending to the family's finances to leading in decision making about the kids' education to the physical upkeep of the house itself.

2) Does the prospective elder care for his children?

Is the elder's care demonstrable for each individual child? An elder will often be called to tend the individual members of the flock. That was the apostolic model (1 Thess. 2:11–12). A church should expect to observe the same thing in a prospective elder with his own individual children.

3) Do the children submit to their father?

Are they obedient to him? Is it evident that they respect and regard him highly? Or is the relationship characterized by animosity and rebellion? Obviously, the particulars of the situation matter here. It may be that a child is spiritually lost and struggling yet still obedient and respectful to his father. Paul's instruction here does not call for a perfect home and perfect children—none exists. So it's wise to ask if the father is managing the home well in the midst of difficult circumstances. Are his children showing proper respect despite any challenges? And if of reasonable age, do his children behave in ways faithful to Christian instruction (Titus 1:6)?

4) Would the children say that their father qualifies to serve as an elder?
Age and understanding matter here, but if the children are old enough to understand the decision at hand, it's worth considering whether they would support their father as worthy of the office. What grounds would they give for affirming or denying a man's qualification? Sensitivity is required. But what our children see in us is likely to be what the church sees in us, only our children tend to see it first and to see us when we're not wearing our public personas.

5) For single men or married men without children, it is important to know about their attitudes toward children and child rearing.
Is a man opposed to having children, or is he postponing having children (if married) for some period of time? In that case there may be selfish tendencies shaping his life. For single men, it might be worth considering whether the man has other opportunities for shepherding children that serve as a proxy on this issue. Does he volunteer with any ministries or community programs that serve youth? Does he have nieces and nephews? Does he volunteer to care for children of other families in the church? If so, how do the children in those programs respond to him, and how does he care for them? Workplace relationships may also provide a similar proxy.

CONCLUSION

The Lord requires that his churches be managed by men who know how to supervise and nurture his children. To a great extent, that is the task of pastoral ministry. Where do we find these men? Where else but at home taking care of business? May the Lord be pleased to raise up men faithful to their homes and gifted for the noble task.

17

MATURE AND HUMBLE

He must not be a recent convert, or he may become puffed
up with conceit and fall into the condemnation of the devil.

1 TIMOTHY 3:6

✛

Have you ever heard the phrase "the zeal of a new convert"? People
use that phrase to describe someone who is boiling over with
enthusiasm because of newfound beliefs or commitments. It's a bit
of a cliché, but the phrase helpfully describes many new believers.
Recent converts tend to have a great deal of energy and enthusiasm. They are bright-eyed and bushy-tailed (to use another cliché).
In many ways, it's wonderful to behold.

Of course, their zeal is not always matched by their wisdom.

For this reason, the Lord insists that any under-shepherd who
leads his church "must not be a recent convert, or he may become
puffed up with conceit and fall into the condemnation of the devil"
(1 Tim. 3:6). The apostle gives us both the qualification and the
rationale.

THE QUALIFICATION

"He must not be a recent convert." That is, the elder must not be a
new believer. Literally, he must not be "newly planted" in the faith.
Like a tender shoot, a new convert will be unable to withstand the
steady trampling that comes with pastoral ministry. His faith must
not be new but aged, like a mature vine producing ripe fruit.

New believers resemble children. Their new life encourages

and excites us, but we must simultaneously recognize that new life is vulnerable. New believers need time to be instructed, shaped, and cared for. And since they are the ones who need such care, they lack the maturity to provide pastoral-level care to others.

The Lord is good to explain this in his Word, and the church does well to heed it. The tendency in some churches—particularly those eager to get people plugged in—is to press new converts into service wherever the first shoots of interest sprout up. But churches should take care not to place a man in a setting that's beyond his ability. Again, they don't want to deprive a man of the care and instruction that he needs. For instance, a church should make sure that a man has good facility in the basics of the faith even before asking him to teach young children.[29]

The potential elder must not be a recent convert to the faith. A recent convert has much to learn, apply, and master in his own life (Rom. 12:1–2) before he can begin to disciple and shepherd others in this way. Paul does not give us an age requirement or length of time that automatically signals maturity. We all know Christians who have been Christians for decades but lack the spiritual maturity requisite for eldership. And conversely, we have probably met a number of people who spiritually were born old and evidence remarkable maturity for their Christian age. Patient discernment is needed. What we want to see is consistent maturity in life and thought over time.

THE RATIONALE

Churches should search for spiritual maturity because of the particular danger associated with immaturity. An immature man "may become puffed up with conceit and fall into the condemnation of the devil." Pride and demonic condemnation, two very dangerous spiritual foes, threaten the spiritual novice.

Pride causes us to think more highly of ourselves than of others. It affects how we treat the sheep, perhaps even tempting us to treat them harshly. It also makes us unwilling to follow other leaders.

Ultimately, a proud man becomes vulnerable to falling in the office, leading to "the condemnation of the devil." "The condemnation of the devil" could refer either to (a) the same judgment which the Devil received for his pride, or (b) the slander and accusation of the Devil, who loves to accuse the brethren. Either way, inviting a novice to the office of elder invites him to onslaughts from within (pride) and from without (judgment).

Calvin summarizes the issue well: "Novices have not only impetuous fervour and bold daring, but are also puffed up with foolish confidence, as if they could fly beyond the clouds. Consequently, it is not without reason that they are excluded from the honour of a bishopric, till, in process of time, their proud temper shall be subdued."[30]

QUESTIONS AND OBSERVATIONS

Pride wears many faces. It is a hydra-headed monster. So diagnosing both pride and immaturity requires great skill and patience.

1) When was the man converted? Is the potential elder a new Christian?

If the man is a new Christian, he is not qualified for the post. He may be a man with great zeal and a desire to serve, but it is better to disciple and train him for a life of godliness. Delay considering him for eldership.

2) If a man has been converted for some time, how spiritually mature is he?

By spiritual maturity, we must not think age or number of years as a Christian. How evident is his conformity to Christ (Phil. 2:5–11)? Does the man demonstrate Spirit-filled living, bearing the fruit of the Spirit (Gal. 5:22–26)? Does he respond with kindness, patience, and compassion in varying situations? Or is he a young man with maturity beyond his years? Such a man should be considered as long as he is mature.

3) To what extent is the man given to pride?

Does the man express awareness of his pride? Does he appear blind to conceit? Or does he fight his pride like a Christian by opening his life to others and submitting to them? Is there any evidence that the office of elder may tempt him to arrogance and exalting himself over others? Consider the man's leadership experiences in other places. Does he evidence pride in those settings? Would his employees or coworkers regard him as a humble man or a puffed-up man?

4) One measure of pride might be overconfidence in the face of spiritual temptations and dangers.

When warned about the accusations and temptations of the Evil One against elders, does he show godly concern or too much sureness of his own ability and strength? Is he gripped with a sense of his own inadequacy (2 Cor. 2:16) and need for God's spiritual protection? A man who is blind to his need for spiritual protection, and who does not vigilantly watch over his life, will soon find himself with a dull heart and vulnerable to the Evil One's attacks.

5) Is the man sensitive to criticism?

Certainly not every criticism a person receives is accurate or warranted. But how will we know whether criticisms are accurate or are unjust, if we refuse to consider them in the first place? Is the prospective elder especially prone to defend himself when criticized? Does he interpret every disagreement as opposition? Pride sometimes manifests itself in an "untouchable" attitude toward the critiques, criticisms, and observations of others. But a humble, poor-in-spirit attitude prayerfully receives such comments as an opportunity for reflection and growth.

6) Ask both the man and others if he is able to submit to others (especially other elders) even when he holds a different opinion.

Can he submit to others when he disagrees with them? A crucial part of an elder's work is knowing how to submit to other biblically qualified, gifted, and Spirit-filled men who will, from time to time, see a matter differently. It's proud to think this will never happen, and it's proud to think the other elders should always submit to you. On a related matter, it's worth asking a prospective elder whether he thinks each of the existing elders is in fact biblically qualified and duly called. If he does not, he may find it difficult to submit to and support their ministries.

CONCLUSION

In looking for reliable men, we cannot afford to minimize the importance of spiritual maturity and humility. Maturity and humility go a long way in protecting the church and the elders from the devices and schemes of Satan.

18

RESPECTED BY OUTSIDERS

Moreover, he must be well thought of by outsiders, so that he may not fall into disgrace, into a snare of the devil.

1 TIMOTHY 3:7

⊕

What do you suppose is the most frequent criticism lodged against the local church and Christians? Consider these common criticisms:

- The church is not doing enough to address real problems (youth, homelessness, etc.).
- The church and Christians are not open-minded; they are backward and discriminatory.
- The church and Christians—especially preachers—are out for your money.
- If the church has the truth, why are there so many divisions and denominations?
- The church is obsolete and unnecessary, and Christians are dangerous to society.
- The church and Christians are boring, not exciting, killjoys, dead.
- Christians are self-righteous and mean.
- The church is full of hypocrites.

Let's face it. Many of these critiques are on target—at least for some churches and professing Christians.

- There *are* Christians who are self-righteous and mean.
- There *are* Christian preachers and churches who care more about money than people.

- There *are* Christians and churches that remain stubborn and close-minded, stuck in bygone eras and unable or unwilling to engage contemporary society with biblical truth.
- Christians *are* a quarrelsome lot. We divide sometimes over the most insignificant things.

It won't do to just ignore such criticisms. Yes, the people who raise them are likely hypocrites themselves. But we *expect* to find hypocrites in the world. The question is: Should we expect such hypocrisy in the church? It may be that our critics have done us a service by pointing out these things. So do we agree with them? If so, what should we do?

A FINAL QUALIFICATION

The apostle Paul comes to his final qualification for elders or pastors: "Moreover, he must be well thought of by outsiders, so that he may not fall into disgrace, into a snare of the devil" (1 Tim. 3:7).

It turns out that what unbelievers think of us really does matter, especially for potential elders. A man who desires to be an elder must possess a strong reputation among those outside the church. These outsiders—people who are not Christians—corroborate or rebut a potential elder's testimony. In most circumstances, the opinion of outsiders must be positive. It might even be said that neutral opinions are not enough, since "he must be *well thought of*." If a man is well regarded inside the church but poorly regarded by non-Christians, he does not qualify as a suitable candidate for Christian ministry.

This qualification has serious spiritual implications. A poor outside reputation, if warranted, means that a man is vulnerable to falling into disgrace or a trap of the Evil One. How many such men have tarnished the witness of their local church, the name of Christ, and the gospel? The Enemy of the elect loves few things more than seeing men fall on their swords because of bad living and poor reputations.

By good outside reputation, however, the Bible does not mean that potential elders will not bear the reproach that Christ bears. The world hated Jesus, and the world will hate his followers (Matt. 10:24–25). The apostles became "the scum of the world" in their time and culture (1 Cor. 4:13). Thus it will be for godly men in every Christ-denying age. "Indeed, all who desire to live a godly life in Christ Jesus will be persecuted" (2 Tim. 3:12). So, the key question is: Does reproach fall upon him because of Christ or because of his own character and habit of life?

Elders must commend the gospel and everything that conforms to sound doctrine. Even the Christian's enemies should feel ashamed about their evil comments in the face of a life lived well for Christ (1 Pet. 3:16). This is the kind of men we should ask God for when it comes to the office of elder.

QUESTIONS AND OBSERVATIONS

1) Does the prospective elder engage with the wider community?
A prospective elder should be salt and light in the world (Matt. 5:13–14). That will be reflected, in part, in the non-Christian relationships he maintains and the civic and community contributions he makes. Does he have any substantial contact with outsiders?

2) What do the prospective elder's non-Christian neighbors and coworkers report about him?
How do outsiders think of him? Do they witness what they would consider Christian or un-Christian behavior in the prospective elder? Do they hold him in high regard? Would any be surprised to hear he is a leader in his church?

3) Is there evidence that the outsiders' opinions are accurate or inaccurate?
It is improbable that Paul intends for the local church to receive the opinions of non-Christians without reflection and discernment. Paul himself would not be judged by any man when that judgment was unfounded and where faithfulness was demonstrable (1 Cor. 4:1–4). Likewise, the local church should neither dismiss the opinion of outsiders regarding its leaders nor indiscriminately swallow

any charge brought against a man. As with all the qualifications, current elders and churches need patient discernment.

CONCLUSION

The call to serve Christ as an under-shepherd is a high calling. Not everyone may take the mantle of leadership in the church. Those who are called must be examples to the flock in every area of life (1 Tim. 4:12). They must be models of devout faith inside and outside the church, commending Christ and the gospel to all. And yet, apart from being able to teach, the qualifications in 1 Timothy 3 are characteristics that every Christian should increasingly possess by God's grace and the work of his Spirit. May the Lord be pleased to grant us the blessing of faithful, reliable men to lead our churches, as well as the fruit of his Spirit.

PART THREE

WHAT GOOD
PASTORS DO

19

ELDERS REFUTE ERROR

He must hold firm to the trustworthy word as taught, so that
he may be able to give instruction in sound doctrine and also
to rebuke those who contradict it.

TITUS 1:9

⊕

I have been an elder or pastor at three churches now, and through
9Marks I have met and spoken with hundreds of pastors. Still, this
is my first tour of duty as a senior pastor.

On the one hand, a senior pastor has the same basic tasks as an
assistant pastor or a lay elder. There's preaching, teaching, counseling, prayer, hospitality, modeling, encouraging, rebuking, and
so on. On the other hand, the leadership demands are different.
More issues stop at my desk for decision, input, and direction.
People seem to see a "The buck stops here!" sign hanging on my
office door. This in turn constantly reminds me that I am not a savior and that I need to be aware of my limitations—limitations now
more visible and influential on the congregation.

Some Christians think the Bible says little about a pastor's or
an elder's routine and duties. Many point to the apostles in Acts 6
and limit the elders' role to teaching and praying. But it's a serious
error to overlook God's instructions in the Pastoral Epistles. They
are a treasure trove of divine instruction for both new and experienced shepherds. Paul opens 1 Timothy 4 with these words:

> Now the Spirit expressly says that in later times some will depart
> from the faith by devoting themselves to deceitful spirits and

teachings of demons, through the insincerity of liars whose consciences are seared, who forbid marriage and require abstinence from foods that God created to be received with thanksgiving by those who believe and know the truth. . . . *If you put these things before the brothers, you will be a good servant of Christ Jesus, being trained in the words of the faith and of the good doctrine that you have followed.* (1 Tim. 4:1–3, 6)

After listing the qualifications for church officers in chapter 3 and indicating that he had listed them so that Timothy would "know how one ought to behave in the household of God, which is the church of the living God, a pillar and buttress of the truth" (v. 15), Paul turns first to address the matter of false teachers.

Timothy—and every elder who desires to be a good minister—must put before the brothers instruction concerning deceitful spirits, the teaching of demons, and the insincerity of liars. These are serious matters: "some will depart from the faith" and devote themselves to evil spirits and their deceptions. Their lies will ravage the soul. In other words, pastors must realize that the Enemy is set on invading the camp and luring defectors to torture and death.

Notice that the apostle Paul treats false teaching as a pastoral matter, not an academic one. He's not interested in having men engage in dispassionate debates about suppositions, propositions, and otherwise equal positions. Ideas have consequences, and 1 Timothy 4 says that our congregations will pay these consequences when they devote themselves to deceitful spirits and the teachings of demons.

This is terrifying! People whom we love and take to be sisters and brothers in the faith may fall prey to spiritual forces of darkness in these later times. While we should not be surprised by this sad turn of events, we should work against it and mourn deeply when it happens. Nothing is more pastoral than protecting our people from such soul-threatening deception and error.

What is a good pastor or elder to do? He must instruct the people about falsehood. "He must hold firm to the trustworthy word as taught, so that he may be able to give instruction in sound doctrine and also to rebuke those who contradict it" (Titus 1:9). I believe this has several implications for a pastor's work.

WHAT IS REQUIRED TO REFUTE ERROR

1) A good pastor must know who and what his people listen to and the extent to which they devote themselves to it.
Deceiving spirits operate through human means, masquerading as ministers of light (2 Cor. 11:13–15). So, elders must encourage their people to learn from genuinely godly and theologically sound teachers.

Which authors does the congregation most read, and what theological commitments do those authors hold? What radio and television ministries command the congregation's attention and why? Do those teachers give evidence of genuine godliness and gospel priorities in their preaching and in their lifestyles? Are those teachers transparent and accountable? Regarding our people's devotedness to any particular teaching, how much time do they spend consuming those ideas? What life decisions are they making based upon those ideas? Do those teachers rival the influence and authority entrusted to the local congregation's elders? More importantly, do any of our people show evidence of rejecting the faith because of the influence of such teachers? Have we lovingly and solemnly made them aware of the error and the consequences that follow from false and unsound belief?

Elders must "give instruction in sound doctrine" and "rebuke those who contradict it." Paul probably has in mind teachers in the Cretan church itself. But in our day, the invasion more likely comes through electronic and print media, which makes the pastor's job a little more challenging.

2) A good pastor must not shy away from identifying falsehood and calling people to avoid it.
Christians can be too polite. And, generally, we are polite about the wrong things. We tend to think that great charity and liberty are important in doctrinal matters, but narrowness and resolute-

ness are demanded in debatable social and public policy issues. We are pleased to "call names" when it comes to politicians, but generally we shy away from doing so when it comes to a minister or preacher. Deny the Trinity? It is simply a matter of academic liberty or personal interpretation. But cross the picket line on taxes, and prepare to be tarred and feathered. Paul tells us to "watch out for" and "avoid" those who cause divisions with damnable heresies (Rom. 16:17–18; Gal. 1:6–8; Eph. 4:14; Titus 3:10–11). That means identifying falsehoods and those who spread them!

Pastors need courage in this matter. Not every sermon need be a jeremiad or screed against some teacher or teaching. In fact, most sermons should not be. But where and when it matters, the shepherd must use the crook to thump the wolf.

3) A pastor must not weaken the seriousness of the apostle's teaching by downplaying the plainly identified demonic source of false teachers and teaching.
Sometimes leaders appear too embarrassed to speak of the Devil and evil spirits. We hear the devotees of scientism telling us that we are backwards and unenlightened. But the light of God's Word shines squarely on Satan, the accuser of the brothers, as the source of this evil. We serve no one by pretending that Satan does not exist. He does. And he wreaks havoc on those blinded to his devices. "We do not wrestle against flesh and blood, but against the rulers, against the authorities, against the cosmic powers over this present darkness, against the spiritual forces of evil in the heavenly places" (Eph. 6:12).

4) A pastor must help his people train their consciences by the Word of God.
The chief characteristic of false teachers identified in 1 Timothy 4 is a seared conscience, a conscience cut off from godliness and goodness. Our people not only must avoid having a seared conscience themselves but must also learn how to recognize such a conscience in the teachers to whom they listen.

The book of Jude offers a pretty good exposé of such teachers, calling them lewd, rejecters of authority, sexually immoral, carnally minded, self-corrupting, money-hungry, lustful, flatterers, mockers, divisive, and ungodly. Our people must recognize these attributes in order to remain safe from grievous wolves (Acts 20:27–28). The Lord gives gifted men to the church to instruct, correct, and train, precisely to teach them such discernment, to help the church know how to spot such wolves even when the faithful elders are absent.

"Put these things before the brothers," says Paul. In other words, teach the people with such clarity that the teaching feels like a physical, tangible object placed within their reach. Good pastors do this by "being trained in the words of the faith" and following good doctrine. As pastors think, believe, and live according to "the pattern of sound words," their people will have a living picture of vibrant faith (2 Tim. 1:13).

5) A good pastor must pray that the Lord would sanctify him and his people in the truth.
If a pastor does this, he follows the greatest example possible. The Chief Shepherd prayed for sanctification in the truth in his High Priestly Prayer: "I do not ask that you take them out of the world, but that you keep them from the evil one. They are not of the world, just as I am not of the world. Sanctify them in the truth; your word is truth. And for their sake I consecrate myself, that they also may be sanctified in truth" (John 17:15–17, 19). Robert Murray McCheyne concluded that the people in his charge needed nothing more from him than his holiness. Perhaps McCheyne grasped something of Jesus's own heart. Jesus sanctified himself for the disciples so that they would be sanctified in the truth. The sanctifying truth that Jesus had in mind was the truth of God's Word. The Savior prayed, "Your word is truth" (John 17:17). And so, those who follow the Chief Shepherd as under-shepherds must pray for Word-produced sanctification for themselves and the people in their charge.

CONCLUSION

There is the danger of being so concerned with error that we fail to preach the truth. Our sermons must not become rants against the latest error or our favorite theological hobbyhorses. But neither should we preach as if the gospel is the only theological option in front of people. Instead we must draw careful distinctions, keeping in mind both gross and subtle errors. We must set the gospel of Christ over and against non-Christian ideas on the one hand, and raise nuances that clarify the gospel against imitations on the other. Nearly every book of the New Testament contains some warning against falsehood and false teachers, making it plain that such teachers and teaching are part of the ongoing warfare between God's people and the enemies of God. A good pastor will set these things before his people and fight for their devotion to Christ and to the truth instead of to deceitful spirits and the teachings of demons.

20

ELDERS AVOID MYTHS AND TRAIN FOR GODLINESS

Have nothing to do with irreverent, silly myths. Rather train yourself for godliness.

1 TIMOTHY 4:7

In 1 Timothy 4:7 the apostle Paul set down a straightforward contrast. He instructs young Timothy to completely avoid "irreverent, silly myths" on the one hand, and to "train himself for godliness" on the other.

The word translated "myths" in the ESV is rendered "old wives' fables" in older versions such as the King James. In using this phrase Paul does not speak pejoratively about either age or gender. Rather, the word refers to untrue and unhistorical tales or fables used for teaching or instruction. The New Testament always uses the word to indicate lying fables, falsehoods, and pretenses—dangerous and erroneous ideas with harmful impacts on people. Here the apostle is warning against myths and fables used for deception.

Timothy, and the good elder, must have nothing to do with such myths. He must refuse any myths begging to be heard.

HOW CAN AN ELDER AVOID MYTHS?

1) A good pastor must make sure he has truthful conversation partners.

Pastors live a great deal of their lives inside their minds. So we who are pastors should make sure that we are not merely listening to ourselves, repeatedly rewinding and playing the tape of our thoughts—our own myths and fables—without assessing and changing them. A good pastor needs a steady diet of truth, not fable. The surest way to achieve this is through the dedicated and focused study of the Scriptures, where eternal truth is preserved and revealed. But a pastor should also dedicate himself to actively reading solid, time-tested classic works of godly saints, always holding those up to the light of Scripture as well.

2) A good pastor must excuse himself from myth and fable.

The pastor must refuse all forms of lying, gossip, half-truths, innuendo, exaggeration, embellishment, dirt, hearsay, talebearing, and slander. Christian circles sometimes resemble non-Christian circles when it comes to these things. Given how often Paul spoke against sins of the tongue, he must have frequently experienced them, too (Eph. 4:25, 31; 5:4; 1 Tim. 3:11). Our consecration includes our separation from water-cooler chatter. The ears of the pastor should be like tombs for myths and fables. Otherwise, as Charles Spurgeon points out, the pastor or elder will become crippled in the ministry:

> It is the extreme of unwisdom for a young man fresh from college, or from another charge, to suffer himself to be earwigged by a clique, and to be bribed by kindness and flattery to become a partisan, and so to ruin himself with one-half of his people. Know nothing of parties and cliques, but be the pastor of all the flock, and care for all alike. Blessed are the peacemakers, and one sure way of peacemaking is to let the fire of contention alone. Neither fan it, nor stir it, nor add fuel to it, but let it go out of itself. Begin your ministry with one blind eye and one deaf ear.[31]

3) A good pastor must not break the confidences of his people.

He should be trustworthy with the truth. He should use a lot of discretion in deciding when, what, how much, and with whom to share information about the ministry and about the congregation. This is not to say that a pastor leads a life of secrecy or swears complete confidentiality, as if he were a clinical psychologist or secular counselor. It means he needs to be discerning and to recognize that souls are in his care, that reputations are in his hands, and that even if he speaks factually and accurately, the transmission of what he says to others might be corrupted. A good pastor does not promise confidentiality where sin and illegal activity are concerned. But also he should not be a talebearer contributing to the rumor mill and the strife that flows from it (Prov. 22:10).

The pastor's job primarily involves speech and words. So a pastor must realize what a great temptation gossip will be. Perhaps we should regularly ask our fellow elders if we have betrayed any confidences, spoken any myths or fables, or shared too much accurate information. Pastors need accountability in this area.

4) A good pastor traces error back to its roots.
This was Jonathan Edwards's twenty-fourth resolution: "Resolved, Whenever I do any conspicuously evil action, to trace it back until I come to the original cause; and then, both carefully to endeavor to do so no more, and to fight and pray with all my might against the original of it."[32] When examining the errors of our lives, we should ask, "Does the error spring from a fable or a myth, or from a truth wrongly applied?" And we should direct our energies to renewing our minds in these things so that purity increasingly inhabits our thinking.

SOME STEPS FOR TRAINING IN GODLINESS

Instead of giving way to fables, Paul instructs Timothy to exercise or train himself for godliness. *Godliness* is a word that needs to be recovered in Christian circles. More importantly, true godliness itself—true devotion or piety toward God—needs reviving and spreading. Godliness is true biblical religion, a pious and morally good life animated by a Spirit-given affection for the Savior.

In his letters to Timothy, the apostle uses "godliness" four times, including its occurrence in our present passage. Each of these instances provides a helpful way to think about striving for godliness. Drawing from the three other passages, we see that we pursue godliness when we do the following three things.

1) *Pray for civil authorities and leaders.* "First of all, then, I urge that supplications, prayers, intercessions, and thanksgivings be made for all people, for kings and all who are in high positions, that we may lead a peaceful and quiet life, godly and dignified in every way" (1 Tim. 2:1–2). Our prayers for those in authority actually affect our freedom and ability to live godly lives. Now, it's easy to believe that rulers and governments hinder godliness. However, the opposite is also true. The effective prayers of the saints for those in authority yield—by God's grace—conditions for the flourishing of godliness.

2) *Combine true piety with contentment.* Paul tells us that "there is great gain in godliness with contentment" (1 Tim. 6:6), which means that godliness comprises one-half of the formula for "great gain." As we develop godliness we must also cultivate contentment. It is hard to imagine lasting godliness apart from genuine contentment. Without contentment, dissatisfaction, murmuring, and complaining will eventually erode the gains of godliness. As pastors, we must guard against such erosion by coupling true piety and affection for God with contentment in the providence of God.

3) *Anticipate persecution* (2 Tim. 3:12). All who would live godly in Christ Jesus shall see persecution. Suffering is a fact of the Christian life. Godliness so distinguishes the Christian from the world that pressure inside the church and persecution outside naturally follow. We train ourselves in godliness by not wilting in the face of persecution. As pastors, we must remember that we do not deserve better treatment than the Savior received. If he was mocked, beaten, and cursed, why should we expect better for following him (Matt. 10:24–25)?

While we anticipate persecution, we must also remember that the Lord knows how to deliver godly men from trials (2 Pet. 2:9). Exercising ourselves toward godliness includes preparing for persecution in the full confidence that no one can pluck us from the Father's hand (John 10:28–29). We do not fear those who can destroy the body and do nothing else; we fear him who can destroy both body and soul in hell (Matt. 10:28). We do "not love [our] lives so much as to shrink from death" (Rev. 12:11 NIV). Such a posture produces godliness.

CONCLUSION

Silly myths and wives' tales focus us not only on this life but on its most trivial aspects. They make us so earthly minded that we are no heavenly good. Better thoughts are required of the Lord's under-shepherds. Let us furnish our minds with material suitable for a heavenly life.

21

ELDERS HOPE IN GOD

We have our hope set on the living God.

1 TIMOTHY 4:10

⊕

We pastors face constant temptation to do pastoral ministry in our own strength and wisdom. We are invited on so many occasions to be men of strength and spiritual courage that we begin to believe that such strength and courage are matters of self-exertion. We may imagine ourselves mustering enough willpower to push our way to any goal.

But this brief phrase from Paul's letter confronts every pastor with the question, Where have we put our hope?

Sometimes we place hope in our study and preparation. Sometimes we place our hope in books read and the convincing arguments they contain. Other times we place hope in relationships, in the affection we share with others in the body. Or we place hope in our articulate expression, clever counsel, and good sermons. Our hope soars when things go well, when people seem pleased with our performance.[33]

All of these hopes are deadly temptations! All of them fade, weaken, and disappoint.

Where can lasting hope be found in life and in ministry? The only sure and abiding bedrock for hope is the living God, "the Savior of all people, especially of those who believe" (1 Tim. 4:10).

THE FREEDOM OF HOPE IN GOD

In all his doing, the good pastor avoids the trap of trusting in his own efforts. In Paul's view of pastoral ministry, hoping in the living God is what animates and strengthens the good pastor, not hoping in himself. The pastor's hope lies in God, and he finds his strength there. The good pastor has the Lord as his portion, refuge, banner, strong tower, and shield. Daily, moment by moment, he runs to the living God.

A good pastor must not let his study and preparation blur a clear vision of the Savior. He must not study to impress others but to see Jesus in all of his crucified humiliation and resurrected splendor. He must open the Word in faith, believing that God is and that he rewards those who seek him (Matt. 6:33; Heb. 11:6). He must open the Scriptures to listen, not to dead words but to a living God who ever speaks through his Word. The good pastor studies in order to teach so that, in teaching, the Spirit may tune everyone's ears to the Master's voice. Before a pastor prepares to preach, he must recognize that he is but a sheep himself, who needs to hear the Chief Shepherd's voice (John 10:3–4, 14–16). A pastor's study and preparation should be, in the best sense of the word, devotional. Does our study reveal personal hope in the living God?

To put our hope in the living God means finding true hope in a living personal relationship. We certainly find encouragement and hope in relationships with the congregation. But, above all, the good pastor must nurture his fellowship with God.

Are our relationships in the church the kind of relationships that foster deeper hope in God, or do they lead us to dependence upon man? Are we agents of encouragement directing others to the living God, on whom they are to rest their hopes? Does our preaching remind others that they have put their hope in the living God who shall never leave them or forsake them? Or does our preaching encourage people to hope in man-made devices, techniques, and therapies? In our lives together, we must continually point out where true hope rests—in Jesus.

What freedom this should give us! Hope in God frees the shepherd from the temptations of false hopes and self-reliance. Hope in God frees us from the "savior complex" that assumes every problem must be fixed by personal wisdom or effort. It frees us from the drudgery of trying to please everyone. It frees us from the bondage of the "success" or "performance" syndrome. For freedom Christ has set us free (Gal. 5:1), and that freedom rests solely and securely on the foundation of hope in Christ. Christ Jesus saved the pastor, and Christ Jesus must save others. Christ gives the shepherd true hope, and Christ must give true hope to his people.

To be good pastors, we must remind our people of this simple yet profound truth: "we have our hope set on the living God." This phrase deserves a full exposition, an exposition written in the actual lives of those who have so trusted the Savior. A good pastor's life should be such an exposition. He should live as one who has (past tense) settled his hope in the Author of life—the one who has life in himself, the giver of eternal life, the living God, Christ Jesus our Lord.

Stop and think for a while: where are you resting your hope?

22

ELDERS COMMAND

Command and teach these things.

1 TIMOTHY 4:11

Sharon stood four feet, ten inches tall. She dressed professionally and spoke with a tender voice. She was a middle-aged mother of two. Despite all the signs of a joyful domestic life, people did not trifle with Sharon. She did not suffer foolishness lightly, and you always had the sense that you should straighten up in her presence.

I worked with Sharon for nearly a year before I learned she had served for several years as a county sheriff. She explained that all the cadets learned a command posture, which in many cases taught citizens to honor the authority officers represented. Whenever an officer actually issued a verbal command, the spoken command simply gave words to what was already implicit in the officer's command posture.

In 1 Timothy 4:11, Paul uses strong language to address a young, perhaps timid Timothy. If Timothy would be a good servant of Christ, he must "command and teach."

The word *command* quickly troubles modern ears. Our culture recoils at authority, especially authority exercised with certainty and strength. We would rather have a leader who facilitates, builds consensus, or motivates. And these latter leadership styles have their place. The wise leader knows when a soft approach is best, when delegation makes sense, and when consensus building must be done.

Nevertheless, in 1 Timothy 4:11 the apostle strikes a different tone for Timothy. He says, "Command . . . these things." A note of authority must be heard in Timothy's interaction with the congregation.

WHAT DOES NEW TESTAMENT COMMANDING LOOK LIKE?

To be sure, Paul is not telling Timothy to go against what Jesus said about Christians' not lording it over one another (Luke 22:25–26). He doesn't mean for Timothy to establish a little dictatorship inside the church where he would govern with an iron glove.

However, a good leader does exercise authority. He will command certain things. Christ Jesus taught as one who had authority, not like the scribes (Mark 1:22). Following the Lord's example, faithful pastors, too, must *command* things. They must teach with authority, not like the hair-splitting scaredy-cats afraid to land on one side of the fence or the other. A good pastor trumpets a clear and certain sound.

But the ability to command is not rooted in the pastor himself. The pastor's talents and abilities are not the grounds for his authority. Neither does the pastor's moral superiority provide the grounds for his authority. The Word of God provides the only sufficient grounds for pastoral authority.

Paul understood this. He wrote to the Thessalonian church saying, "For you know what instructions we gave you *by the authority of the Lord Jesus*" (1 Thess. 4:2 NIV). The good pastor must learn that in commanding things, he himself is not the commander. He is but a messenger and an example. The commands are not his to develop and distribute at whim. The commands must clearly be from the Lord. This is why "and teach" is so vital in Paul's instruction. Timothy commands *by teaching* the already delivered commands of Christ (Matt. 28:18–20).

Moreover, the good pastor will major on things of great importance. "These things" of verse 11 concern spiritual warfare in which the Christian engages and also the freedom provided in

Christ. "These things" refers to godliness, sound doctrine, and a firm trust in the living God, the Savior of believers. Timothy—and all good pastors—should major in these things.

What prevents good pastors from commanding as they should? Calvin insightfully identifies one challenge:

> The doctrine is of such a kind, that men ought not to be weary of it, though they hear it every day. There are, no doubt, other things to be taught; but there is emphasis in the demonstrative *these*; for it means that they are not things of small importance, of which it is enough to take a passing and brief notice; but, on the contrary, that they deserve to be repeated every day, because they cannot be too much inculcated. A prudent pastor ought, therefore, to consider what things are chiefly necessary, that he may dwell on them. Nor is there reason to dread that it shall become wearisome; for whosoever is of God will gladly hear frequently those things which need to be so often uttered.[34]

Why should an elder dread repeating instruction from God's Word? One reason is that the fear of man whispers to us, "Your people have already heard this. They grow tired of your saying the same things." We fear the opinions of others, and that may drive even our teaching behavior.

Yes, they have heard it. But it's unlikely that they have adopted the teaching perfectly. Seasoned elders and pastors know that fruitful teaching demands repetition. All too often we Christians look in the mirror only to turn away and forget the image we saw (James 1:23–24). As Ken Sande puts it, "Christians leak."

CONCLUSION

It should not be burdensome for a pastor to repeat and re-teach (Phil. 3:1). And pastors should not shrink at the faces of men who give outward or spoken disapproval. We pastors command these things because the commands of the Lord are good and not burdensome (1 John 5:3) for the health of the people in our care, and in order to faithfully discharge our duty as good servants of Christ.

23

ELDERS LET NO ONE DESPISE THEIR YOUTH

Let no one despise you for your youth.

1 TIMOTHY 4:12

✠

Some pastor search committees will not consider a man younger than age forty. Of course, that would have meant the end of Timothy's candidacy, not to mention Jesus's. Then there are those committee members who look at a young pastor and conclude, "He's young but we'll train him and fit him to our tastes." There are also members of churches who disregard a pastor's instruction because "he is so young and inexperienced." Most people with these attitudes have never served as elders or trained to be pastors.

In a million ways youth can be despised. What young pastor does not know the frustration of trying to lead older members who resist his leadership, not because they recognize errors in his understanding of the Scripture but because they very broadly and generally regard themselves as older and wiser? Now, Paul does not call Timothy to neglect the accumulated wisdom of older members and leaders. A humble Timothy would wisely take full advantage of what older saints offer. Nonetheless, Paul instructs Timothy not to wrongly capitulate to other people's estimation of his youth. His age is not a barrier to leading the church and being a good pastor. Youth is not an impediment to godliness, maturity, and leadership ability in the pastor.

SOME IDEAS TO AVOID DESPISING YOUTH

First Timothy 4:12 is written to Timothy, but it has application to young and old alike.

1) Older pastors should be willing to give opportunity and to take risks when it comes to younger pastors.

Older pastors should not hold against their younger peers something that cannot be changed (age), especially since God does not hold it against them. Rather, they should encourage, instruct, support, and train such young men as Paul did Timothy. This will inevitably mean giving the young pastor room to act and lead.

2) Young pastors should not be brash and unteachable.

A young pastor should not respond to those who despise his youth by, in turn, despising their agedness or by becoming a sulking, cantankerous brat. That would only confirm the bias and make the task of leading all the more difficult. Instead, the young pastor must remain humble, patiently living with the people while faithfully discharging all his duties.

3) Young pastors should not adopt an attitude of defeat in the face of people who despise their youth.

Young pastors should not hang their heads, murmur, or complain. They should square their shoulders, lock their eyes on Christ, and bid all to follow them as they follow Christ. I often witnessed Mark Dever, senior pastor of Capitol Hill Baptist Church in Washington, DC, point the way forward, disdain distraction, and push toward the mark when others resisted his leadership. That could be frustrating for some people around him, but humble steadfastness serves both pastor and people. Young pastors simply must continue following Jesus.

Perhaps you are a young pastor facing this kind of difficulty. Beloved, you must not quit. You must not shrink. You must not murmur and pout. You must "command and teach." It is interesting that Paul's instruction in verse 12 follows the rather strong word to "command" in verse 11. Likely he knew about the fear of man and the tendency to cave in that reside in young ministers.

CONCLUSION

The younger a man, the more hesitant he may be to lead with authority commensurate with the authority of God's Word and the pastoral office. This instruction calls Timothy to man up, to grow up, to lead in such a way that his age is no predictor at all of his ability, godly confidence, and dependability as a pastor. It is what a good young pastor must do.

24

ELDERS SET AN EXAMPLE

But set the believers an example in speech, in conduct, in love, in faith, in purity.

1 TIMOTHY 4:12

✠

College teammates and fans nicknamed him "The Round Mound of Rebound," paying homage to both his portly shape and his backboard-crashing prowess. When he was a professional, fans selected him as an NBA all-star eleven times. He earned two Olympic gold medals for his part on the Dream Team in 1992 and 1996. In 2006 the Naismith Memorial Basketball Hall of Fame inducted him into its hallowed ranks. He was recognized as one of the fifty greatest players in NBA history.

The NBA even included him on its All Interview team for each of his thirteen years in the league. He spoke colorfully. He spoke aggressively. He spoke loudly. He spoke all the time. To this day, Charles Barkley owns the most ironic professional moniker I have ever heard. It's simply "Sir Charles."

He never claimed royal pedigree, and his behavior proved it. Barkley frequently found himself in outbursts on and off the court, once spitting at a fan in retaliation for racial slurs.

One thing Sir Charles Barkley never claimed to be was a role model. In 1993 Nike launched an ad campaign featuring Barkley defiantly arguing that athletes are not role models. The ad stirred national controversy. But Barkley insisted that parents should be role models and should stop looking for young professional athletes to provide patterns for youth behavior and values.

With Charles Barkley's rejection of the idea in the early 1990s, the notion that celebrity equals role model fell on hard times. Perhaps I belong to the last generation encouraged to look up to and emulate role models. But even if the idea has vanished from public discourse, it certainly has not vanished from Scripture.

ARE PASTORS THE LAST ROLE MODELS?

One thing a good pastor must do is set an example to the believers. He is to be a role model. This is a simple yet incredibly important statement. It is so important, that God set it down in the eternal truths of the Scripture.

The principal way that Timothy avoids having his youth held against him is to be an example to all the believers. Paul charges him to live a life worthy of emulating, observing, and following. Paul's instruction pushes up the bar of pastoral ministry far above the inconsistent and trivial examples presented by professional athletes.

Who is sufficient for these things (2 Cor. 2:16)? Setting this kind of example is a daunting task. It requires the supernatural grace and empowering of God.

Paul in effect says that the pastor *is supposed to* live his life in a fishbowl, with outside eyes fixed upon his swimming patterns and eating habits. He lives, not behind a curtain or blinds, but behind see-through glass.

Most people, of course, naturally tend toward privacy, the comfort and anonymity of home, and a kind of interiorness that prefers the world of ideas and thoughts. But 1 Timothy 4:12 calls pastors out of themselves and their comfort onto the stage of pastoral example-setting.

WHAT DOES PASTORAL EXAMPLE-SETTING ENTAIL?

1) A good pastor's example is set for the believers.

That may sound obvious, but perhaps no other occupation is so often regarded as an example for *everyone*—Christians and non-

Christians. Gratefully, Paul does not say that here in 1 Timothy 4:12. Any man attempting to be an accessible example for all the world will twist himself into a salty pretzel!

Pastors are called to set examples for their own churches. Their example-setting is primarily local and primarily for believers. What the unbelieving world desires from pastors inevitably conflicts with what Jesus Christ requires of them and what the saints need to see. So pastors must be clear about who makes up their audience—the local congregation in their charge, not believers abstractly, generally, or universally. Paul grounds this instruction in the gritty, real-world context of a relationship between a particular pastor and a particular congregation of people.

The apostle's instruction means that a pastor should take stock of his particular social and historical context. When I was in Washington, DC, I learned that a pastor needs to show his congregation how to set appropriate priorities (God, family, work) since the entire city seems to order life the opposite way (work, family, God). When I lived in the southeastern United States, where nominal Christianity remains strong, I learned that a pastor needs to be an example of discernment and clarity, doctrinal fidelity, and speaking the truth in love. Audience and context matter. The pastor must keep that in mind as he sets an example.

2) A good pastor's example makes him accessible.

By this I do not mean he shows little control over his calendar or fails to place appropriate walls around his family. The demands of the pastorate necessitate such control. But this command to Timothy does suggest that the pastor is around the people, with the people, tangible to the people. He must be observed, and that cannot be done if he is not in some sense before the people. He will likely need to be seen in various arenas: at fellowship events, at lunch or dinner, at home, in others' homes, and so forth. What is the right amount of accessibility? Each man must consider his circumstances to answer that question. But, in principle, a good pastor must be accessible enough to effectively set an example.

3) There are particular areas in which a good pastor must set an example.

I am glad for Paul's list of actions and virtues here in verse 12, not because I have reached the mark, but because it keeps me from being overwhelmed and unsure of where to start. He lists five things: speech, conduct, love, faith, and purity. It's a weighty list, but it helps us to know where example-setting is necessary.

What we say must be exemplary. Among other passages, Ephesians 4:25, 29, and James 3 provide principles for a pastor's pattern of speech. A pastor must listen longer; speak truthfully and disclose fully (not to be confused with exhaustively); be direct and loving (open rebuke is better than secret love); speak what is necessary and what edifies; and administer grace to his hearers.

What we do must be exemplary. A good pastor's conduct will be seen by all. It will either confirm, call into question, or deny the authority and power of the gospel. A good pastor lives in a manner worthy of his calling and imitates God (Eph. 4:1; 5:1; Phil. 1:27; 4:1). The startling reality for every pastor is that his life and manner of being will inevitably and steadily impress itself on the character of his congregation. A congregation will generally take on the pastor's manner. And a pastor's impress will not easily be smoothed out by even the next two or three pastors that follow. Subsequent pastors will either be jostled and tossed over the bumpy, hardened mud tracks left plowed into the people or will find the path smooth and the way straight because of the previous pastor's example in speech and conduct.

Our love must be exemplary. Here is a place where our example, set before the saints, also testifies to the unbelievers around us (John 13:34–35). For our love to be exemplary, we must follow the example of Jesus, whose love is supreme. He gave himself for his people. He was born that he might die. He voluntarily took upon himself the afflictions of his people. He bore the scorn, ridicule, mocking, and beating that we deserve, and faced the omnipotent and infinite wrath of the Father in our place. He entered into our suffering and countenanced our temptations. He identified with us in every way as a suitable high priest. Now, we too must set an example of self-sacrificing love!

The good pastor sets an example *in faith*. Self-reliance is an abomination in a pastor. Faithlessness is a pox on his ministry. A good pastor trusts in God. The elder must fix his hope on the God who cannot die, who has life in himself, who cannot lie, who is the God of truth. The congregation should be able to witness their elders' faith in the whole range of life situations: elation, tragedy, conversion, apostasy, support, opposition, abundance, lack, fruit, and barrenness. In high times and low, a good pastor bases his life and decisions on the certainty of Jesus's love, lordship, sovereignty, and goodness.

A good pastor sets an example *in purity*. Purity in the pulpit must stir up and point the way for purity in the pew. How easy it is for a pastor to hide filth. He can, if he wishes, isolate himself, fabricate an identity for the public, and live a double life. He may, if he chooses, speak much about purity and holiness and deny the power thereof. A good pastor is to labor, toil, and strive (1 Tim. 4:10) for godliness, knowing that "godliness is of value in every way, as it holds promise for the present life and also for the life to come" (v. 8).

The beauty of purity and holiness ought to seize the heart of the pastor, so much so that he disdains all alternatives. Christlikeness motivates him. He constantly desires to enter into that pure loveliness of Jesus, and he is troubled when his desire grows cold. He sets an example in purity because he knows the blessing of purity. He knows what true beauty is and depends upon God to live it before the people—in his entertainment choices, his music preferences, his modesty, his devotion, his confession, his regard for younger women (1 Tim. 5:2), his study of art and literature, his adoption and critique of style, and so on. Bob Kauflin sums it up well:

> Jesus came to purify his people once and for all through his atoning sacrifice (Titus 2:14). He fulfilled what ceremonial purification could only point to. But God's demand for purity hasn't

changed. The Lord is still holy. So it is not surprising that God wants leaders in the church to set an example for the believers in purity.

Purity is the quality of being undefiled, unmixed, and undiluted, free from evil or contamination. The first area this applies to is our motives. God calls us to guard against being "led astray from a sincere and pure devotion to Christ" (2 Corinthians 11:3). Leading worship for financial gain or public recognition dishonors God. God wants our worship to be sincere, not hypocritical; willing, not forced; wholehearted, not distracted. In other words, pure.[35]

CONCLUSION

Pastors and elders "set the believers an example in speech, in conduct, in love, in faith, in purity" by God's grace and omnipotent aid. Churches develop reverence for the Lord and for the pastorate when pastors live such imitation-worthy lives. In his kindness, God promises great reward to those men who give themselves to this noble task (1 Pet. 5:1–4).

Charles Barkley was correct: professional athletes are not this kind of role model. Only the Spirit-empowered servants of Christ are.

25

ELDERS TEACH

*But set the believers an example in speech, in conduct, in
love, in faith, in purity.*

1 TIMOTHY 4:12

⊕

If you had to boil pastoral ministry down to one thing, what would
it be? Surely, we cannot easily boil it down to one thing. Even the
functions we have considered from 1 Timothy defy answering this
question simply. But if you could, what would it be?

A case could be made for "set the believers an example" in all of
life. Jesus told his disciples that he set an example they should follow (John 13:15). Elsewhere, the apostle Paul exhorts, "Follow my
example, as I follow the example of Christ" (1 Cor. 11:1 NIV). He tells
the Philippians the same thing (Phil. 3:17). And in 1 Timothy 4:12
Paul encourages Timothy to be an example in speech and conduct.
Perhaps being an example is one way of describing a good pastor.

Another way of bottom-lining what a good pastor does, however, is to consider what function the example plays. At root, setting an example is teaching. A good pastor teaches. "Command and
teach these things" (1 Tim. 4:11). "Until I come, devote yourself to
the public reading of Scripture, to exhortation, to teaching" (v. 13).

PASTORAL DEVOTION

So what should a good pastor do? He should devote himself to
these three pursuits: public reading of Scripture, exhortation, and
teaching. The word translated "devote" implies private preparation

beforehand. The private candle-burning of personal study fuels the public ministry of a good pastor. But this study must be sanctified as well. Charles Bridges writes:

> The tree of knowledge may thrive, while the tree of life is languishing. Every enlargement of intellectual knowledge has a natural tendency to self-exaltation. The habit of study must be guarded, lest it should become an unsanctified indulgence; craving to be fed at the expense of conscience or propriety; employed in speculative enquiries, rather than in holy and practical knowledge; preoccupying the time that belongs to immediate duties; or interfering with other avocations of equal or greater moment. A sound judgment and a spiritual mind must be exercised, in directing these studies to the main end of the Ministry. Let none of them entrench upon those hours, that should be devoted to our study of the Bible, or our preparation for the pulpit.[36]

THREE DISCIPLINES FOR A PASTOR DEVOTED TO TEACHING

A good pastor devotes himself to teaching in three ways.

1) Public reading of Scripture. Many churches I have attended seem impatient with hearing God's Word read publicly. One suspects that people have grown accustomed to *not* hearing God's Word read publicly except in the briefest snippets. Appetites for hearing God's Word have grown quite small.

Some find the public reading of Scripture boring. Others think it gets in the way of the "real worship"—singing. Some do not understand it or have difficulty following along. Perhaps you've heard these and other reasons for neglecting public Scripture reading. Do you think the Lord is impressed by any of them?

The Father reveals himself in and through his Word. The Word points to Jesus. The Spirit moved men to write it. Given the Trinitarian effort, what good reason could we have for neglecting it?

Paul tells Timothy to "devote yourself" to public reading of Scripture—for good reason. The Word brings life. Every revival recorded in Scripture followed the recovery of the public reading of God's Word. For example, Moses read the Book of the Covenant with the people in Exodus 24:7. Joshua read the entire law at the renewal of the covenant following the fiasco at Ai in Joshua 8. The great scene in Nehemiah 8 featured reading and expounding the Scripture all day long (Nehemiah 9; 13). Repentance was Jeremiah's hope when he urged Baruch to read the Word before the people (Jeremiah 36). And how many times in the Gospels does the Lord begin some great statement with, "Have you not read. . . "?

A good pastor devotes himself to making sure the Word of God remains central in the public gathering of the people, in part, through the public reading of Scripture. This reading shapes God's people and is itself both an act of teaching and the basis for other instruction.

2) Exhortation. A good pastor also exhorts from God's Word. He challenges his people not only to hear the Word but to heed the Word, to put the Scripture into effect in their lives. He exhorts by encouraging, rebuking, correcting, warning, and comforting (1 Tim. 3:16–17). He moves his people to feel and to act based upon God's Word.

The apostolic model of pastoral ministry focused on applying the Word to people individually (1 Thess. 2:8–13). Reading is helpful but not sufficient. An elder must apply it to the several spiritual conditions gathered in the assembly. Some need nursing, others a rod, still others a precision cut. A good pastor endeavors to let the Word minister to each need by reading and applying.

3) Teaching. Elders teach both by reading and by exhorting. However, sheep that are growing also require systematic instruction. Timothy is to devote himself to doctrine. Paul will have none of that high-sounding sophistry about "doctrine divides" or "it's about a relationship, not doctrine." There can be no relationship without knowing to whom we are related. Timothy's habit must be to build doctrine by amassing the truths of Scripture into a whole for his people. He must teach, for apart from teaching he cannot be a good pastor.

PUTTING IT INTO PRACTICE

From Bridges's wise counsel, we may note several applications for the faithful elder:

1) Guard the hours needed for reading and for studying so that effective teaching might occur.
2) Read widely on some level, but deeply when it comes to Scripture and theology.
3) Regularly read systematic, biblical, and historical theology. Respectively, this will teach you the Bible's whole teaching on a subject, the themes and narrative of Scripture, and how other faithful saints have dealt with these issues, thereby avoiding the pride that refuses to learn from others.
4) Discipline your thinking by writing out your sermon manuscripts, at least if you're a young preacher. Not every pastor needs this discipline. But for many, preaching from a manuscript adds precision and order to our sermons.
5) Surround yourself with people who give honest, constructive feedback on the sermons. You might meet with other pastors or elders, listen to others' sermons, or use staff meetings as an opportunity for co-laborers to encourage, correct, and help.
6) Have an overall approach to public teaching that coordinates the pulpit, mid-week Bible study, Sunday school, small groups, and other teaching opportunities. Everything cannot be done from the pulpit, so other opportunities should be used strategically.
7) Share teaching responsibilities with others, if possible. Pastors need help and should actively enlist gifted men in the leadership and in the congregation to help carry the load.

CONCLUSION

What is a good pastor to do? In a word: teach. Through his words and his deeds, he teaches the sheep. Let us sanctify our study and preparation that we may fully and skillfully feed God's sheep from the manna of his Word. It is God's Word that gives life. A good pastor believes this, trusts this, and centers his ministry on this fact.

26

ELDERS GROW

Practice these things, immerse yourself in them, so that all may see your progress.

1 TIMOTHY 4:15

✠

Morning after morning, they rushed to the windowsill, anxious to see if their plant had grown. Their science teacher had tasked them with planting a seed in a small transparent plastic cup filled with rich, dark soil, and they were to document its growth from a small seed nestled in the soil to a shoot and eventually to a plant.

My two daughters were captivated by the mystery of burgeoning life. Every day they riveted their attention to the plant. I remembered having the same fascination as a child their age when my class completed the same project.

All living things grow. Nothing reveals vitality and strength like proper growth. Perhaps that is why everyone desires and welcomes growth. We find pleasure and encouragement wherever we find growing things. God hardwired growth into life, and now we seek it in every area.

PASTORS MUST GROW

The apostle Paul uses strong words with Timothy to drive home the encouragement to grow. He calls Timothy to "devote" and "train" himself so that his growth will affirm spiritual life and vigor.

The idea of devotion appears several times in this chapter. Some will be devoted to "deceitful spirits" (v. 1), while Timothy should be devoted to public Scripture reading, exhortation, and teaching. Moreover, Timothy is to "train" himself—toil and strive—in godliness (v. 7). The image of sweaty exertion jumps off the page.

Ministry is labor. It's work. If we approach it wanting ease and convenience, we will be run over and flattened by the rushing traffic of responsibility, hardship, difficulty, sin, disappointment, apparent failure (ours and others'), death, disease, and all the other things that accompany fallen human life. Ministry is labor.

Like any labor, pastoral ministry requires routine, trial, and improvement. Paul teaches Timothy to "practice these things," referring to the things mentioned in the previous verses:

- warning the people of false teachers;
- avoiding false doctrine and myths;
- training himself in godliness;
- hoping in the living God;
- commanding and teaching;
- keeping his head up as a young pastor;
- setting an example in life;
- public reading of Scripture, exhorting, and teaching;
- and using his gifts.

At the end of this litany, Paul tells Timothy to practice and devote himself to everything on the list.

Both the text and our experience suggest that some of these things will not come naturally to pastors or elders. We might be capable of some things but find others difficult. If we expect everything to be easy, we will despair of ever being fruitful. If we expect everything to be difficult, we may never try and so neglect our gifts and calling, and miss the opportunity to see God's grace in both success and trial. A good and godly focus on the correct things is crucial.

One way to maintain a proper focus is to realize that ministry takes practice. It takes concentration, meditation, action, and evaluation. And good practice requires strong devotion.

Anyone with a child who at one time begged to play a musical instrument knows that the child's devotion to practicing the instrument after the newness wore off was critical to his or her success. Likewise, my high school basketball coach always chimed, "You play the way you practice." You can guess that he made sure our practices were rigorous affairs. We probably watched as much film of our practices as we did of our games. We were to be focused, prepared, on task, and always ready to be corrected. All of that is a part of practice. If we take a lackadaisical attitude toward practice, our ministries will stall, lag, falter, and decay, and we will not win the prize due to our lack of necessary preparation, focus, and evaluation.

THE DISCIPLINE OF PRACTICE

A few disciplines may serve us in our effort to be good shepherds.

1) Approach the study as though it were the game. The study is not optional. We will pastor the way we practice. In the study, we run the routines and plays that make our game-time performance smooth, efficient, and effective. When my study is off, eventually so is the rest of my game. My counseling is not as sharp or rigorously biblical as it should be. I find myself at a loss for how to respond to things I should know. When my study is off, my discipling of other men tends to be shallower, my preaching more self-reliant and wrongly emotional. I can preach to some effect, deliver more-or-less wise counsel, and come alongside men. But my lack of preparation will eventually show up in the "game" of their real lives. I may be eloquent, but I will not be useful. A good elder needs to approach the study as though it were game time, because game speed in ministry requires focused, prepared, and well-coached players.

2) Find yourself a good coach. There is no deserted island like that of pastoral ministry. Many pastors experience loneliness in pastoral ministry; others get on just fine with their own company. But for all of us, the deserted island creates a most tragic condition: little or no evaluation of our work. We are left to the cruel clutches of self-evaluation. Few of us offer balanced appraisals of ourselves. We are prone to fall off one side or the other—either everything is great and everyone else needs to get on board, or everything is terrible and the sky is falling. Neither is accurate.

A good coach will give us unvarnished but loving feedback on our habits of thinking, our preaching, our counseling, and our lives. In order to practice, as Paul tells us to do in verse 15, we need to "watch film" with someone who knows the plays and can point out strengths and weaknesses. A humble pastor seeks that kind of feedback.

3) Cultivate humility. Cultivating humility is harder than it sounds. As we noted earlier, pride is a hydra-headed monster that asserts itself in so many ways and at so many times. Conquering pride can feel a little like trying to nail Jell-O to a wall. To help in this battle, take C. J. Mahaney's book *Humility: True Greatness* in hand and study it thoroughly.

Search your region intentionally and carefully for men who are evidently and universally regarded as humble. They are probably not leading the new, hip, fast-growing church in the area. They are probably laboring quietly in relative anonymity, which may be why they exhibit such humbleness of heart. Cultivate humility by watching these men, following them as they follow Christ, and confessing your pride. Neither practice nor coaching will aid us if we are not humble, teachable, and able to receive and use godly feedback.

THE BENEFITS OF A PASTOR'S PROGRESS IN THE FAITH

A good pastor or elder does all of this, we are told, "so that all may see [his] progress." God means to display a pastor's growth for the benefit of the sheep. Church members look to their pastors, like children rushing to a windowsill in search of budding life, to see growth and be encouraged by it. His growth benefits them in several ways.

1) If everyone sees the pastor's growth, it suggests that his people were already aware of some of his imperfections and flaws. A good pastor must delight in that! Allowing others to know that he is not perfect liberates him from unrealistic expectations and makes him human to the congregation. He can go on with the project of being a fallen creature redeemed by grace. So he should not cover his faults. Wisely, with godly edification in view, he should confess them. He should let the people know that he had a life before Christ and that since coming to Christ he has discovered how much he needs to grow in grace and holiness. They know that. He should remind them of it, and in most cases he will find added liberty and grace—especially if the congregation receives the same grace from its pastors.

2) If pastors are allowed to make progress in Christian living, pastoral burnout and pressure may be avoided. When congregations practically demand perfection from their pastors, they unwittingly force pastors into ministerial failure or ministerial hypocrisy. A pastor can either admit his weaknesses and be written off, or he can hide his weaknesses by wearing a mask of perfection. Men crash and burn in either situation. The third and biblical way is to allow the pastor to be human—warts and all—while praying and hoping for his growth. Through this third way congregations keep good pastors, and good pastors pursue Jesus.

3) When a good pastor is encouraged to make progress in the faith, his congregation improves their ability to see signs of trouble in his life. Growth is normal in the Christian life, and that is no less true for the good pastor. If pastors are not growing over time, fellow elders and leaders should explore potential reasons for stagnation. There should be fervent prayer for a reversal of course. Pastors should consult good books like Don Whitney's *Ten Questions to Diagnose Your Spiritual Life* or Octavius Winslow's *Personal Declension and Revival of Religion in the Soul.* In addition, a good pastor should work to make sure that the church's budget reflects this desire for growth by granting the pastor the opportunity to attend several good conferences a year and by including a good book budget to fill out his library and reading diet.

4) A good pastor's growth is to be seen. "All" are to see his progress (v. 15). This is part of what it means to set a good example. A good pastor wants his people to grow and so he himself should grow. From time to time he should hear his people commend his growth. Now, of course, this means pastors need to stay in one place for a period of time so that people will have time to see his progress in godliness, grace, preaching, spiritual strength, and love.

CONCLUSION

Many Christians feel intimidated by their pastors largely because so many pastors present themselves as supermen with no need for practice or growth. Intimacy between pastor and people requires transparency and the work of God's grace. That can feel like risk if a pastor or a people are proud. But the wonderful benefit is that pastor and people will begin to treat each other with grace, and they'll watch what God-produced growth looks like.

27

ELDERS WATCH THEIR LIFE

Keep a close watch on yourself and on the teaching. Persist in this, for by so doing you will save both yourself and your hearers.

1 TIMOTHY 4:16

In April 2006, I sat in a hotel ballroom shoulder-to-shoulder with three thousand fellow pastors and seminarians at the first Together for the Gospel Conference. It was two and a half days of wonderful fellowship in Christ and his gospel. After the thunderous melody of three thousand men singing rich Christian truth and hearing wonderful sermons on preaching and teaching, C. J. Mahaney closed the conference with a remarkably practical exhortation to watch our lives as pastors. That sermon deserves repeated listening to. In fact, you should probably stop reading this chapter and go straight to the Together for the Gospel website to hear the sermon, or find a copy of *Preaching the Cross* to read it.[37]

C. J. makes the point that pastors are better at watching their doctrine than their lives. So a good pastor needs bifocals to see both his life and his doctrine. Sound doctrine should lead to right living. It does not always do so, but the inconsistency is evidence that we need to be vigilant in both areas—to *closely* watch doctrine and deed. Pastors are to truly live the Christian life until both belief and action conform to the Word of God.

WATCHING LIFE AND DOCTRINE

How might pastors watch both life and doctrine?

1) A good pastor surrounds himself with quality men who help him watch his life.

Accountability is essential—and not just passive, reactionary accountability but searching, probing, initiative-taking accountability. Pastors need people to ask the tough questions that are avoided in normal conversation, to pursue us rather than merely to listen to us. Elders need Christian friends whose agenda for our holiness is at times more zealous than our own (Prov. 27:17; Heb. 10:24). Elder or pastor, can you list three to five men who have open access to your life?

2) A good pastor maintains a healthy interest in, participation in, and love for his family.

Many pastors face the temptation of making an idol of either family or ministry. As strange as it sounds, an inordinate love for ministry and ministry activity reveals the pastor's lack of affection for God himself. But if his affection for and obedience to the Savior are strong, he will be very affectionate toward his family. First Timothy 3:4–5 establishes family care as a prerequisite for ministry and therefore a priority over ministry. So a good pastor watches his life by watching the ordering of his priorities when it comes to his family. He develops the ability and habit of saying no to worthy ministry opportunities in order to say yes to his family. "Perhaps nowhere are we so liable to self-deception, or so little open to conviction, as in the management of children."[38]

3) A good pastor keeps close watch on his thought life.

He fights against anger, jealousy, censoriousness, lust, and the like. He works to think about those things that are lovely, true, and of good report (Phil. 4:8). Too often pastors listen to themselves rather than speak to themselves. If we are not careful, we believe what we tell ourselves and end up living ill-informed lives. To watch his life closely, the pastor must fight sin at the level of thoughts and desires, planting godly seeds and plucking out thorns and weeds before they choke his life.

4) A good pastor protects himself, his family, and his church from sexual immorality and the appearance of evil.

A good pastor knows not to make any provision for his flesh nor to leave his life open in such a way that invites unwanted attention, advances, or confusion. He does not meet or travel alone with women. He is not a shoulder to cry on for vulnerable women. His office is open or within view, avoiding the cloak of secrecy. A wise pastor makes his administrative assistant and his wife aware of meetings with women. Moreover, he actively and joyfully gives himself to his wife in intimacy. He gouges out his eyes, cuts off his arms, and whatever else is necessary to protect himself, his family, and his church from immoral acts. He humbly and eagerly involves others in this protection and accountability.

5) A good pastor watches his life for rest and recreation.

There should be adequate rest in the calendar and appropriate recreation. To be sure that he gets rest, a pastor should invite feedback on his schedule and habits. Eventually, pastors lose the battle and the war if they do not rest. If Jesus does not return soon, a life of pastoral ministry will be a long, slow labor. To thrive, a pastor needs to take care of his physical needs.

Charles Bridges maintained a long ministry in England in the mid-1800s. He understood the necessity of rest and recreation. "The devoted servant of God will find a measure of relaxation in the turning from the more painful to the more soothing exercises of his work. Some total diversion will however occasionally be needed. And let him not suppose that his Master requires labour, when both his body and spirit demand rest. A wise management of diversion will tend rather to strengthen, than to enervate, the tone of his spiritual character, and the power of his Ministry."[39]

6) A good pastor watches habits or idiosyncrasies that come from his strengths.

Sometimes a pastor's strength is also his weakness. Martyn Lloyd-Jones warns of this in his classic *Preaching and Preachers*:

> Watch your natural gifts and tendencies and idiosyncrasies. Watch them. What I mean is that they will tend to run away with you. It can all be summed up in a phrase—watch your strength. Not so much your weaknesses: it is your strength you have to watch, the things at which you excel, your natural gifts and aptitudes. They are the ones that are most likely to trip you because they are the ones that will tempt you to make a display and to pander to self. So watch these; and also your idiosyncrasies. We all have these, and we must watch them.[40]

Overplaying our strengths may weaken other aspects of our ministry. We may become lobsters with one giant claw we use for everything while our other miniature claw receives little use and attention. Over time, it may be that our strengths create the imbalance as much as any weakness.

CONCLUSION

Watching our lives and our doctrine does not come naturally. This is why the faithful pastor must exercise discipline. He must become a student of his heart and his mind. And he must invite others to inspect the corners he cannot see.

28

ELDERS WATCH THEIR DOCTRINE

Watch your life and doctrine closely. Persevere in them,
because if you do, you will save both yourself and your hearers.
1 TIMOTHY 4:16 (NIV)

✠

I am not sure what people mean when they call someone a "heresy hunter," but I am pretty sure I am one. It has to do with my own conversion. Having been committed to Islam at one time, I came to Christ perhaps a bit hyper about doctrine and theology. From the beginning I was driven to read sound doctrinal works. I did not know the term *doctrine* or have a coherent sense of what I was looking for other than accurate knowledge of God. Imagine how my heart jumped when on the first weekday following my conversion, I visited the local Christian bookstore, made my way to the theology section, and purchased two books—J. I. Packer's *Knowing God* and Martyn Lloyd-Jones's three-volume work, *Great Doctrines of the Bible*.

I had no idea what I was buying, but I have not been the same ever since purchasing and reading these classic works. The Lord showed me tremendous grace in leading me to these men and their work, starting my Christian life on sound doctrinal footing. I am ever so thankful.

Having known what it is to believe and base my life on a lie, I am something of a heresy hunter. Now, by that term, I do not mean I am the type who searches under every rock for any error, however small, in order to slam the person and his error with all my might. Neither am I angry and vengeful when it comes to error. But I am seriously concerned by it. My personal sojourn affirms the importance of Paul's admonition: "Watch your life and doctrine closely" (1 Tim. 4:16 NIV).

HOW ARE WE TO WATCH OUR DOCTRINE CLOSELY?

1) Make Scripture central.

A good pastor is a man of one book. He knows no higher science than theology, and no richer art than the study of Scripture. The holy Word of God occupies center stage in his thinking. He drinks deeply from the Scripture, and hears Paul's admonition: "Do not go beyond what is written" (1 Cor. 4:6 NIV). He closely watches his doctrine by thinking God's thoughts after him in the Scripture.

2) Read and reread good old books.

Without belittling recent books, the older classics are still the best. Classic books typically offer greater rigor, insight, and depth than most of the published works in our mass-market-oriented day. Classic works have survived the test of time. Many people today love C. S. Lewis, the famed writer and Christian thinker who gave the world *The Chronicles of Narnia* and *Mere Christianity*. But few follow Lewis's sage advice on reading. Consider these lines from the opening paragraphs of Lewis's introduction to Athanasius's classic *On the Incarnation*.

> There is a strange idea abroad that in every subject the ancient books should be read only by the professionals, and that the amateur should content himself with the modern books.
>
> This mistaken preference for the modern books and this shyness of the old ones is nowhere more rampant than in theology.
>
> Now this seems to me topsy-turvy. Naturally, since I myself am a writer, I do not wish the ordinary reader to read no modern books. But if he must read only the new or only the old, I would advise him to read the old. And I would give him this

advice precisely because he is an amateur and therefore much less protected than the expert against the dangers of an exclusive contemporary diet. It is a good rule, after reading a new book, never to allow yourself another new one till you have read an old one in between. If that is too much for you, you should at least read one old one to every three new ones.[41]

Reading tested and proven works helps the pastor keep watch over his doctrine.

3) Read bad books once in a while.
Not regularly or exclusively, but on occasion, a good pastor reads a bad book. He may do this because many of his people are interested in the book, or because the book is creating a stir in the larger church world. He may read such a book to know what the issues are and what is at stake in order to better shepherd his people, or to sharpen his own apologetic ministry. In either case, after a full diet of Bible and classics, a faithful shepherd watches his doctrine by familiarizing himself with relevant errors.

4) Read church history and historical theology.
Most of the errors we see have already been made by someone before us. There is nothing new under the sun—including bad theology. A good pastor helps to inoculate himself from such errors by reading church history and historical theology where doctrinal errors are chronicled, debated, and resolved by godly men of earlier generations. There is truth in the old cliché—"Those who do not know history are doomed to repeat it."

5) Avoid novelty and fads.
Most error starts with novelty, with a desire to say something new or innovative. But few faithful teachers want to be doctrinally innovative. Whenever a good pastor comes across something altogether new in his study and reading, he asks at least four questions: (1) Specifically, how does this depart from accepted, established truths of the faith once and for all delivered to the saints?

(2) What impact does this idea or doctrine have on other important doctrinal issues? (3) How does this impact the lives of people? (4) Is this impact really worth the dangers or problems associated with the novel interpretation?

Paul tells Timothy in verse 7 to avoid irreverent, silly myths. The good pastor will follow Paul's counsel. The world clamors ceaselessly for new things. It wants ingenuity and breakthroughs. There is something about the human heart that craves to be an original, to be unique. But great explosions of error occur when a pastor's combustible lust for cleverness and originality mingles with the fuel of worldly desire for novelty.

6) Keep learning from solid teachers.

What good pastor will ever stop learning? And who can master all there is to know from centuries of godly and learned pastors, theologians, and thinkers? A good pastor commits himself to strengthening his knowledge of the Savior and the faith, and he makes a specific plan for such learning. He may take a seminary course (on campus or online), listen by radio or online, attend good conferences, or join a study group. But one way or another he will keep learning.

7) Commit to the church's statement of faith.

Pastors should pledge themselves to uphold and defend the church's statement of faith as an accurate summary of the Bible's teaching. The moment a pastor waivers in his commitment to an article in the statement, he should confess it to his fellow elders and leaders for accountability, correction, and discipline if necessary. In our church, elders "promise that if at any time I find myself out of accord with any of the statements in the Statement of Faith and Covenant I will on my own initiative make known to the pastor and other elders the change which has taken place in my views since my assumption of this vow." This pledge strengthens our doctrinal self-watch. (See the appendix for sample elder ordination vows.)

8) Develop an instinct for identifying doctrinal softness and drift.
In most cases, a good pastor serves as the chief theological officer in the church. Consequently, he needs to be fairly astute at monitoring his own thoughts and being intellectually honest with himself. He needs a nose for identifying theological laziness, sloppiness, or indifference. He needs to fight against any tendency toward doctrinal compromise.

A pastor or elder will not serve his people well if he tends to constantly surrender small plots of theological ground whenever the fear of man surfaces. He must discern whether people-pleasing tendencies are the habit of his heart and whether that weakens doctrinal resolve. He must know whether he tends to avoid conflict and whether that habit erodes his fidelity to the truth. He must know when and how pragmatism assumes control of his thinking such that he is tempted to leave off sound doctrine and choose a thing "because it works." He needs a honed instinct for spotting drift and softness in himself and a specific plan for overcoming it.

CONCLUSION

Every heresy or widespread doctrinal corruption in the church arose while some pastor was on the job. He either introduced it or allowed it into the body. A significant number of such errors were developed by men who sought what was right in their own eyes and disregarded the great truths of Scripture and the godly wisdom of those before them.

Paul's exhortation to watch one's life and doctrine is deeply practical and critically important. The good pastor's close watch affects the spiritual well-being of his people. By watching, he will save both himself and his hearers. May the Lord give us grace to be good and faithful ministers to his people.

AFTERWORD

Obey your leaders and submit to them, for they are keeping watch over your souls, as those who will have to give an account. Let them do this with joy and not with groaning, for that would be of no advantage to you.

HEBREWS 13:17

How should a pastor feel about his pastoral labors? What should be the dominant emotion that characterizes his ministry? Many pastors feel exhausted, frustrated, ineffective, even depressed. They find pastoral ministry a burden.

But what does God intend under-shepherds to feel about their work? Hebrews 13:17 answers the question for us when it says the pastor's work should be a joy. You will often hear pastors say that they feel sobered by that verse's reference to their accountability to God for the souls entrusted to their care. But as sober as the warning may be, joy should pervade the shepherd's labor on behalf of the sheep.

If you are a pastor reading this book, I hope the book's practical exhortations and suggestions increase your joy. I hope focusing on the basics of pastoral character and responsibility aids you in charting a course for your ministry and enjoying the benefit that comes from clarity. The clearer we are on our call, the greater the likelihood of knowing joy in our service.

Or perhaps you're a member of a church, or you participate on a pastoral search committee. Have you thought about your role in making pastoral ministry a joy for the men who serve? Hebrews 13:17 calls you to follow your pastors or potential pastors so they will not be burdened. And did you notice that a joyful minister is an advantage to you as a member, and to the congregation? Your spiritual benefit, by God's design, is tied to your pastor's joy.

So in a very real sense, the pastor and the people live together in such a way that they increase one another's joy. This book can aid your joy or it can be a burden to you as a pastor. I pray that it aids joy rather than causes burdens. For joy, read and apply this book in light of the gospel of Jesus Christ. Christ has become wisdom, righteousness, holiness, and redemption for all who believe (1 Cor. 1:30). Since Jesus alone accomplishes our salvation, pastor and people are set free to pursue faithfulness without burden, and growth with joy. I pray that as you use this little volume, you'll keep the glorious life, crucifixion, burial, resurrection, ascension, and coming of the Lord Jesus Christ in full view. To think of him often and long is itself joy.

Grace, peace, and love in Jesus Christ.
Your fellow laborer in the cause of the Savior.

APPENDIX

Sample Elder Ordination Vows

TO THE ELDER

1. Do you reaffirm your faith in Jesus Christ your Savior, acknowledge him Lord of all and Head of the Church, and through him believe in one God—Father, Son, and Holy Spirit?

   I do.

2. Do you believe the Scriptures of the Old and New Testaments to be the Word of God, totally trustworthy, fully inspired by the Holy Spirit, and the supreme, final, and only infallible rule of faith and practice?

   I do.

3. Do you sincerely believe, receive, and adopt the essential tenets of the faith as expressed in our Statement of Faith, as reliable expositions of what Scripture leads us to believe and do, and will you be instructed and led by the Statement as you lead the people of God?

   I do, and I will with God's help.

4. Do you promise that if at any time you find yourself out of accord with any part of the Statement of Faith, you will on your own initiative make known to your fellow elders the change which has taken place in your views since your assumption of this vow?

   I will.

5. Do you subscribe to the government and discipline of XYZ Church?

   I do.

6. Will you fulfill your office in obedience to Jesus Christ, being continually guided by the Holy Spirit under the authority of Scripture?

   I will.

7. Do you promise to be mutually submissive to your fellow elders in the Lord and will you love your colleagues in ministry, your fellow pastors and staff members—working with them, subject to the ordering of God's Word and Spirit?

   I do.

8. Have you been induced, as far as you know your own heart, to accept the office of elder from love of God and sincere desire to promote his glory in the gospel of his Son?

   I have and I do.

9. Do you promise to be zealous and faithful in promoting the truths of the gospel and the purity and peace of the church, whatever persecution or opposition may arise against you on that account?

   I do, with God's help.

10. Will you be faithful and diligent in the exercise of all your duties as an elder whether personal or relative, private or public, and will you endeavor by the grace of God to adorn the profession of the gospel in your manner of life, and to walk with exemplary piety before this congregation?

    I will, by the grace of God.

11. Are you now willing to take personal responsibility in the life of this congregation as elders to oversee the ministry and resources of the church, and to devote yourself to prayer, the ministry of the Word, and the shepherding of God's flock, relying upon the grace of God, in such a way that XYZ Church and the entire Church of Jesus Christ will be blessed?

    I am, with the help of God.

TO THE CONGREGATION

12. Do you, the members of XYZ Church, acknowledge and publicly receive _____ and _____ as elders as a gift of God to this church to lead us in the way of Jesus Christ?

    We do.

13. Will you love them and pray for them in their ministry, and work together with them humbly and cheerfully, that by the grace of God you may accomplish the mission of the church, giving them all due honor and support in their leadership to which the Lord has called them, to the glory and honor of God?

    We will.

NOTES

1. D. A. Carson and Douglas J. Moo, *An Introduction to the New Testament*, 2nd ed. (Grand Rapids, MI: Zondervan, 2005), 380.

2. Among the useful volumes available, the interested reader might consult: Michael Brown, ed., *Called to Serve: Essays for Elders and Deacons* (Grandville, MI: Reformed Fellowship, 2007); Mark Dever, *A Display of God's Glory: Basics of Church Structure: Deacons, Elders, Congregationalism, and Membership* (Washington, DC: IX Marks, 2001); David Dickson, *The Elder and His Work* (Phillipsburg, NJ: P&R, 2004); Benjamin J. Merkle, *40 Questions about Elders and Deacons* (Grand Rapids, MI: Kregel, 2008); Phil A. Newton, *Elders in Congregational Life: Rediscovering the Biblical Model for Church Leadership* (Grand Rapids, MI: Kregel); Alexander Strauch, *Biblical Eldership: An Urgent Call to Restore Biblical Church Leadership* (Colorado Springs, CO: Lewis & Roth, 1995); and Timothy Z. Witmer, *The Shepherd Leader: Achieving Effective Shepherding in Your Church* (Phillipsburg, NJ: P&R, 2010).

3. Interested readers may find the May/June 2010 issue of the *9Marks eJournal* useful in understanding this aspect of the deacon's role. The ejournal may be obtained at http://www.9marks.org/ejournal/deacons.

4. D. Martyn Lloyd-Jones, *Victorious Christianity: Studies in the Book of Acts*, vol. 3 (Wheaton, IL: Crossway, 2003), 236, 237–38.

5. John Bunyan, *Pilgrim's Progress in Modern English* (Lafayette, IN: Sovereign Grace, 2000), 47.

6. Philip Graham Ryken, *1 Timothy*, Reformed Expositors Commentary (Phillipsburg, NJ: P&R, 2007), 124.

7. George W. Knight III, *The Pastoral Epistles: A Commentary on the Greek Text* (Grand Rapids, MI: Eerdmans, 1992), 170.

8. Ryken, *1 Timothy*, 128–29.

9. For a very good treatment of this theme see Witmer, *The Shepherd Leader*, especially chaps. 1–2. See also Timothy S. Laniak, *Shepherds after My Own Heart: Pastoral Traditions and Leadership in the Bible* (Downers Grove, IL: InterVarsity, 2006).

10. Since the Bible uses these titles as synonyms, we use them that way in the sections that follow.

11. For an excellent defense and biblical exposition of authority and love, see Jonathan Leeman, *The Church and the Surprising Offense of God's Love: Reintroducing the Doctrines of Church Membership and Discipline* (Wheaton, IL: Crossway, 2010), especially chaps. 3 and 7. See also Alexander Strauch, *Leading with Love* (Littleton, CO: Lewis & Roth, 2006).

12. Lemuel Haynes, "The Character and Work of a Spiritual Watchman," in *The Faithful Preacher: Recapturing the Vision of Three Pioneering African-American Pastors*, ed. Thabiti M. Anyabwile (Wheaton, IL: Crossway, 2007), 29.

13. For an excellent examination of godly ambition, see Dave Harvey, *Rescuing Ambition* (Wheaton, IL: Crossway, 2010).

14. Charles Bridges, *The Christian Ministry: With an Inquiry into the Causes of Its Inefficiency* (Edinburgh: Banner of Truth, 1997), 23.

15. William Still, *The Work of the Pastor* (Ross-shire: Christian Focus, 2001), 15.

16. John Calvin, *Commentaries on the Epistles to Timothy, Titus, and Philemon*, trans. William Pringle (Grand Rapids, MI: Baker, 1996), 77.

17. D. A. Carson, "The Role of the Elder," a lecture delivered at Capitol Hill Baptist Church, Washington, DC, May 3, 1998. Audio may be downloaded at http://resources.christianity.com/details/mrki/19980503/80CDCC9C-93C9-43DC-BEDB-365CAF55BD36.aspx. For a lightly edited transcript of the lecture see "Defining Elders" at http://sites.silaspartners.com/partner/Article_Display_Page/0,PTID314526%7CCHID598014%7CCIID2157886,00.html.

18. John MacArthur, *The MacArthur Study Bible* (Nashville, TN: Word Bibles, 1997). See the note on 1 Timothy 3:2, p. 1864.

19. Ryken, *1 Timothy*, 111.

20. For further study, consider John Piper and Wayne Grudem, eds., *Recovering Biblical Manhood and Womanhood: A Response to Evangelical Feminism* (Wheaton, IL: Crossway, 1991); Wayne Grudem, *Evangelical Feminism and Biblical Truth: An Analysis of More than 100 Disputed Questions* (Sisters, OR: Multnomah, 2004); and a host of valuable resources available from the Council on Biblical Manhood and Womanhood at http://www.cbmw.org.

21. Alexander Strauch, *A Christian Leader's Guide to Leading with Love* (Littleton, CO: Lewis & Roth, 2006), 67.

22. Ibid., 99.

23. John Calvin, *Commentaries: Epistle to the Romans* (Grand Rapids, MI: Baker, 1981), *xxvii*.

24. D. Martyn Lloyd-Jones, *Preaching and Preachers* (Grand Rapids, MI: Zondervan, 1971), 109–10.

25. John Calvin, *Commentaries: First Epistle to Timothy* (Grand Rapids, MI: Baker, 1981), 80.

26. See Alfred Poirier, *The Peacemaking Pastor* (Grand Rapids, MI: Baker, 2006).

27. Charles Edward White, "Four Lessons on Money from One of the World's Richest Preachers," *Christian History* 19 (Summer 1988): 24; cited in Randy Alcorn, *Money, Possessions and Eternity* (Sisters, OR: Multnomah, rev. ed. 2003), 298–99.

28. Ryken, *1 Timothy*, 116.

29. So while Paul raises this issue especially with elders, it may be prudent to apply this more broadly in the church by encouraging new converts and members to complete appropriate theological and ministry training before involving them in a particular area of service, or by encouraging them to take the first six months of their membership to focus primarily on learning and building relationships in the church.

30. Calvin, *Commentary on 1 Timothy*, 83–84.

31. Charles Haddon Spurgeon, *Lectures to My Students* (Fearn, Scotland: Christian Focus), 365.

32. Jonathan Edwards, *Memoirs of Jonathan Edwards, A.M.*, vol. 1, The Works of Jonathan Edwards (Peabody, MA: Hendrickson, 1998), *lxiii*.

33. For a helpful discussion of these temptations, see Kent and Barbara Hughes, *Liberating Ministry from the Success Syndrome* (Wheaton, IL: Crossway, 1987).

34. Calvin, *Commentary on 1 Timothy*, 13; emphasis original.

35. Bob Kauflin, *Worship Matters: Leading Others to Encounter the Greatness of God* (Wheaton, IL: Crossway, 2008), 47.

36. Bridges, *The Christian Ministry*, 49.

37. Mark Dever, J. Ligon Duncan III, R. Albert Mohler Jr., and C. J. Mahaney, *Preaching the Cross* (Wheaton, IL: Crossway, 2007).

38. Bridges, *The Christian Ministry*, 166.

39. Ibid., 137–38.

40. Lloyd-Jones, *Preaching and Preachers*, 255.

41. C. S. Lewis, "On the Reading of Old Books," in *God in the Dock: Essays on Theology and Ethics* (Grand Rapids, MI: 1970), 200.

GENERAL INDEX

alcohol/alcoholism, 31, 32, 83–84, 85; violence and alcohol consumption, 84

Alcorn, Randy, 89

apostles, 20, 111; choice of among to "serve tables" (to deacon), 20; and the inspiration of God's Spirit, 20–21

Athanasius, 156

Barkley, Charles, 135–36

Baruch, 143

Bridges, Charles, 142, 153; guidelines of for putting teaching into practice, 144

Bunyan, John, 27

Calvin, John, 61; on drunkenness, 84; on the teaching of the Scriptures, 78

Carson, D. A., 61

Christians, criticisms lodged against, 105–6

Christlikeness, 52

Chronicles of Narnia, The (Lewis), 156

Chrysostom, 61

commands: ability and call of elders to command, 127–28; New Testament view of commanding, 128–29

deacons, 19–20, 49; choosing of, 23–24; as the early church's "shock absorbers," 21; and generosity, 32–33; and "holding the mystery of faith," 36–37; as problem-solvers, 28. *See also* faith, and deacons; greed, and deacons; questions, for prospective deacons; service to others, and the testing of deacons; sincerity, and deacons; sobriety, and deacons/elders

domestic/marital abuse, 86

elders, 49; appointing of multiple elders in the early church, 49–50; avoidance of myths by, 117–19; elders must be above reproach, 57–58; elders must have the respect of nonbelievers and outsiders to the faith, 106–7; elders must not be recent converts to the faith, 99–100; growth of, 145–47; importance of family leadership abilities in prospective elders, 95–96; nobility of the office of elder, 52–53, 57; paid and unpaid elders, 50; questions and observations concerning prospective elders, 54–56, 59; and the refutation of error, 111–13, 116; stirring up aspiration in elders, 51–52; "super elder" concept, 51; traits to watch for in prospective elders, 53–54, 58–59. *See also* elders, responsibility of for teaching; elders, and sexual fidelity; elders/pastors, requirements for the refutation of error; sobriety, and deacons/elders

elders, responsibility of for teaching, 141; guidelines for putting teaching into practice, 144; pastoral devotion and teaching, 141–42. *See also* teaching, disciplines needed for

elders, and sexual fidelity (being a "one-woman man"), 61–62; questions concerning for married men, 64–65; questions concerning for single men, 63

elders/pastors, growth of, 145–47

elders/pastors, and the refutation of error, 111–13, 116. *See also* elders/pastors, requirements for the refutation of error

elders/pastors, requirements for the refutation of error: pastors must identify the demonic source of false teachers and teaching, 114; pastors must identify falsehood, 113–114; pastors must have knowledge of what their flock listens to and to what extent, 113; pastors must pray for the sanctification of themselves and their flock, 115; pastors must train the consciences of their flock by the Word of God, 114–15

faith, and deacons, 36–37; persevering in faith, 39; questions and observations concerning, 37–39
"For the Love of Money" (O'Jays), 87

gentleness and patience, as qualifications for elders and deacons, 84–85, 86
God, as our Shepherd, 48; determination of God to be our Shepherd, 48–49
godliness, steps for training in: anticipate persecution, 120–21; combine piety with contentment, 120; pray for civil authorities and leaders, 120
gospel, the: truth of, 38; understanding of, 38
Great Doctrines of the Bible (Lloyd-Jones), 155
greed, and deacons, 31–32, 87–88; questions and observations concerning, 32–33, 90–92

heresy hunting, 155–56
holiness, business and purity of, 139–40
hope, 123; and the freedom of hope in God, 124–25
hospitality: example of, 71–72; hospitality enables discipleship, 72–73; hospitality enables evangelism, 72; hospitality expresses care, 72; hospitality expresses love, 72; questions and observations concerning, 73–74; why Christians should value hospitality, 72–73
humility, 148; questions and observations concerning, 101–3; as a requisite for prospective elders, 100–101
Humility: True Greatness (Mahaney), 148

Jeremiah, 143
Jesus Christ: authority of, 128; as the good shepherd, 48

Kauflin, Bob, 139–40
Knowing God (Packer), 155

leadership: of families as a prerequisite to becoming an elder, 95–96; and love, 96–97; questions and observations concerning, 97–98
Lewis, C. S., 156
Lloyd-Jones, Martyn, 155; on a pastor's strengths being weaknesses, 154; on

what churches should require of a teacher of the Scriptures, 81–82

MacArthur, John, 61
Mahaney, C. J., 148, 151
McKenzie, William, 47
Mere Christianity (Lewis), 156
ministry, practice of, 146–47; discipline required for, 147–48
money, love of. *See* greed, and deacons
myths, avoidance of by elders, 117–19

nephalios (Greek: temperate, sober-minded, vigilant), 67

On the Incarnation (Athanasius), 156

Packer, J. I., 155
pastors, 50, 161–62; benefits of a pastor's progress in faith, 148–50; exemplary conduct of, 138; faith of, 139; love of, 138–39; purity of, 139; responsibility of to clarify and teach the goodness of the leadership task, 52; responsibility of to encourage young men to consider being elders, 51–52. *See also* pastors, means of watching their lives; pastors, means of watching their doctrine; pastors, as role models and example setters; pastors, youth of
pastors, means of watching their doctrine: by avoiding novelties and fads, 157–58; by committing to the church's statement of faith, 158; by developing an instinct for identifying doctrinal drift, 159; by learning from reputable teachers, 158; by making Scripture central, 156; by occasionally reading bad books, 157; by reading church history and historical theology, 157; by reading and rereading classic old books, 156–57
pastors, means of watching their lives: a pastor must keep watch on his thought life, 152–53; a pastor must maintain a healthy interest in and love for his family, 152; a pastor must protect himself, his family, and his church from sexual immorality, 153; a pastor must rest, 153; a pastor must surround himself with quality men, 152; a pastor must watch his idiosyncrasies, 154

pastors, as role models and example setters, 135–36, 140; particular areas
in which pastors can set examples,
138–40; pastors as the last role models, 136; pastors' examples should
make them accessible, 137; pastors
set examples for believers, 136–37
pastors, youth of, 131; willingness
of older pastors to take risks with
younger pastors, 132; young pastors
must control brashness and be teachable, 132; young pastors must not
have a defeatist attitude, 132–33
Paul, 31, 42, 62, 131, 166n29; condemnation of polygamy by, 61;
criterion that prospective elders
should be "able to teach," 78–79; on
false teachers, 112; specific advice
to Timothy concerning pastoral
ministry, 146
Pilgrim's Progress (Bunyan), 27
polygamy, 61
Preaching the Cross (Mahaney), 151
Preaching and Preachers (Lloyd-Jones),
154

questions, for prospective deacons: does
the prospect demonstrate Spirit-
inspired wisdom?, 26; does the prospect evidence the fruit of the spirit?,
25–26; does the prospect have a
reputation for being filled with the
Spirit?, 24; does the prospect put the
ministry of Word and prayer above
the practical needs of the church?,
24–25; is the prospect a servant?, 25

Ryken, Philip, 62

service to others, and the testing of deacons, 41–42; questions and observations concerning, 42–43
sexual purity, and Christian witness, 62.
See also elders, and sexual fidelity

sincerity, and deacons, 27–29; questions
and observations concerning, 29–30
sobriety, and deacons/elders, 31; does
the deacon prospect drink alcohol?
32; elders and deacons must not be
"given to drunkenness," 84
Strauch, Alexander, 68

teaching, 84; as a central part of proclaiming the gospel, 77; importance
of in the New and Old Testaments,
77; necessity of, 77–78; as the
primary task of the elder, 78; questions and observations concerning,
79–82. *See also* elders, responsibility
of for teaching; teaching, disciplines
needed for
teaching, disciplines needed for: devotion to teaching and doctrine, 143;
exhortation from God's Word, 143;
public reading of Scripture, 142–43
temperance/temperate people, 67–68;
questions and observations concerning temperance in elder prospects,
68–69
Timothy, 31, 42, 131; public Scripture
reading and teaching of, 145–46
Together for the Gospel Conference
(2006), 151
trendiness, 68–69

violence: against a wife or children, 86;
and alcohol consumption, 84

Wesley, John, frugal lifestyle of and the
importance of tithing, 88–90
White, Charles, 88

SCRIPTURE INDEX

Genesis
2:24   64

Exodus
24:7   143

Leviticus
19:33–34   72

1 Samuel
1–2   96

Nehemiah
8   143
9   143
13   143

Psalms
12:2–3   28
23   48

Proverbs
1:7   24
22:10   119
23:5   92
26:28   28
27:17   152
30:7–9   33

Ecclesiastes
12:14   50

Isaiah
53:6   47

Jeremiah
36   143

Ezekiel
34:1–10   51
34:11–16   48

Matthew
5:13–14   107
5:27–30   63
5:43–47   72
6:19–24   90
6:33   124
9:36   53, 55
10:24–25   107, 120
10:28   121
28:18–20   128
28:19–20   77

Mark
1:22   128
6:34   55
10:45   25

Luke
10:25–37   96
11:1   77
12:15–21   32

John
10:3–4, 14–16   124
10:11   48
10:12–13   50
10:14–18   49
10:28–29   121
13:15   141
13:34–35   72, 138
17:15–17, 19   115
17:17   115

Acts
2:42–47   73
6   20, 23, 111
6:1   20
6:2   20
6:3   21, 23, 24
6:7   21
20:17, 28   49
20:27–28   115
20:28   49

Romans

12:1–2	100
12:13	73
14:1	85
15:5–6	86
16:17–18	114
16:18	28

1 Corinthians

1:30	162
4:1–2	50
4:1–4	107
4:13	107
4:16	156
7:17	62
9:5	62
11:1	141
12:4–11	49
13:13	29

2 Corinthians

1:17–18	28
2:6	102
2:16	136
8:1–5	33, 92
8:7	90
8:9	92
9:8	33
11:3	140
11:13–15	113

Galatians

1:6–8	114
5:1	125
5:22–23	25
5:22–26	101
5:25–26	26

Ephesians

4:1	37, 57, 138
4:3	86
4:11–16	42, 49, 77
4:14	114
4:15	29
4:17–24	62
4:25, 29	138
4:25, 31	118
4:29	29
5:1	138
5:1–2	57
5:3–14	62
5:4	118
5:19	77
5:22–32	65

Philippians

1:27	57, 138
2:3	26
2:3–8	25
2:5–11	101
3:1	129
3:17	141
4:1	138
4:8	152
4:11–13	33

Colossians

1:10–12	57
3:14	29
3:15	86
3:16	77

1 Thessalonians

2:3–6, 10	55
2:5	28
2:7–8, 11–12	96
2:8–13	143
2:11–12	80, 97
4:2	128

1 Timothy

2:1–2	120
3	50, 51, 108
3:1	51
3:1–2	57
3:2	51, 61, 67, 71, 77, 84
3:2–3	87
3:3	83, 84
3:3, 8	88
3:4–5	95, 152
3:6	99
3:7	105, 106
3:8	27, 31
3:9	35, 36
3:10	41, 42
3:11	118
3:12	107
3:13	43
3:16–17	143
4	50, 111, 114
4:1–3, 6	112
4:7	117
4:8	139
4:10	123, 139

4:11	127–128, 141
4:12	52, 57, 108, 131, 132, 135, 136, 137, 141
4:13	141
4:15	145
4:16	151, 155, 156
5:2	63, 139
5:8	90
5:9	58
5:17	49
5:18	50
5:22	54
5:22ff.	42
6:6	120
6:9–10	91

2 Timothy

1:13	115
2:23	85
2:23–26	84
2:24	85
3:12	120
4:3–4	86
4:5	86

Titus

1:5	49
1:6	98
1:7	88
1:9	111, 113
2:2	68
2:2–6	77
2:6	63
2:7–8	69
3:10–11	114

Hebrews

10:24	152
11:6	124
13:7	50, 56
13:17	49, 52, 161

James

1:19–20	26
1:23–24	129
3	138
4:1–3	84

1 Peter

3:16	107
4:8–9	73
5:1–3	49, 57
5:1–4	140
5:2–3	55, 56
5:4	50

1 John

5:3	129

Jude

16	28

Revelation

12:11	121

DOES YOUR CONGREGATION ASK, "WHAT
EXACTLY AM I SUPPOSED TO BE DOING AS
A MEMBER OF THIS LOCAL CHURCH?"

HERE'S SOME HELP.

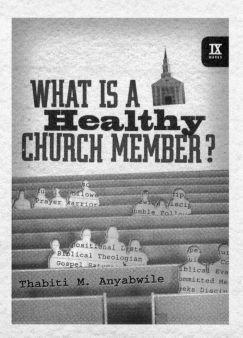

"In an era when Christians seem confused about
what kind of community the church ought to
be, here's a helpful handbook outlining the
church's true biblical priorities, especially as
they apply to individual church members."

John MacArthur, President, Grace to You